EGYPT TWO YEARS AFTER MORSI (PART I)

HEARING

BEFORE THE

SUBCOMMITTEE ON
THE MIDDLE EAST AND NORTH AFRICA

OF THE

COMMITTEE ON FOREIGN AFFAIRS
HOUSE OF REPRESENTATIVES

ONE HUNDRED FOURTEENTH CONGRESS

FIRST SESSION

MAY 20, 2015

Serial No. 114–36

Printed for the use of the Committee on Foreign Affairs

Available via the World Wide Web: http://www.foreignaffairs.house.gov/ or
http://www.gpo.gov/fdsys/

U.S. GOVERNMENT PUBLISHING OFFICE

94–688PDF   WASHINGTON : 2015

COMMITTEE ON FOREIGN AFFAIRS

EDWARD R. ROYCE, California, *Chairman*

CHRISTOPHER H. SMITH, New Jersey
ILEANA ROS-LEHTINEN, Florida
DANA ROHRABACHER, California
STEVE CHABOT, Ohio
JOE WILSON, South Carolina
MICHAEL T. McCAUL, Texas
TED POE, Texas
MATT SALMON, Arizona
DARRELL E. ISSA, California
TOM MARINO, Pennsylvania
JEFF DUNCAN, South Carolina
MO BROOKS, Alabama
PAUL COOK, California
RANDY K. WEBER SR., Texas
SCOTT PERRY, Pennsylvania
RON DeSANTIS, Florida
MARK MEADOWS, North Carolina
TED S. YOHO, Florida
CURT CLAWSON, Florida
SCOTT DesJARLAIS, Tennessee
REID J. RIBBLE, Wisconsin
DAVID A. TROTT, Michigan
LEE M. ZELDIN, New York
DANIEL DONOVAN, New York

ELIOT L. ENGEL, New York
BRAD SHERMAN, California
GREGORY W. MEEKS, New York
ALBIO SIRES, New Jersey
GERALD E. CONNOLLY, Virginia
THEODORE E. DEUTCH, Florida
BRIAN HIGGINS, New York
KAREN BASS, California
WILLIAM KEATING, Massachusetts
DAVID CICILLINE, Rhode Island
ALAN GRAYSON, Florida
AMI BERA, California
ALAN S. LOWENTHAL, California
GRACE MENG, New York
LOIS FRANKEL, Florida
TULSI GABBARD, Hawaii
JOAQUIN CASTRO, Texas
ROBIN L. KELLY, Illinois
BRENDAN F. BOYLE, Pennsylvania

AMY PORTER, *Chief of Staff*   THOMAS SHEEHY, *Staff Director*
JASON STEINBAUM, *Democratic Staff Director*

————

SUBCOMMITTEE ON THE MIDDLE EAST AND NORTH AFRICA

ILEANA ROS-LEHTINEN, Florida, *Chairman*

STEVE CHABOT, Ohio
JOE WILSON, South Carolina
DARRELL E. ISSA, California
RANDY K. WEBER SR., Texas
RON DeSANTIS, Florida
MARK MEADOWS, North Carolina
TED S. YOHO, Florida
CURT CLAWSON, Florida
DAVID A. TROTT, Michigan
LEE M. ZELDIN, New York

THEODORE E. DEUTCH, Florida
GERALD E. CONNOLLY, Virginia
BRIAN HIGGINS, New York
DAVID CICILLINE, Rhode Island
ALAN GRAYSON, Florida
GRACE MENG, New York
LOIS FRANKEL, Florida
BRENDAN F. BOYLE, Pennsylvania

CONTENTS

EGYPT TWO YEARS AFTER MORSI (PART I)

WEDNESDAY, MAY 20, 2015

House of Representatives,
Subcommittee on the Middle East and North Africa,
Committee on Foreign Affairs,
Washington, DC.

The subcommittee met, pursuant to notice, at 10 o'clock a.m., in room 2172 Rayburn House Office Building, Hon. Ileana Ros-Lehtinen (chairman of the subcommittee) presiding.

Ms. Ros-Lehtinen. The subcommittee will come to order.

After recognizing myself and Ranking Member Mr. Deutch from Florida for 5 minutes each for our opening statements, I will then recognize other members seeking recognition for 1 minute. We will then hear from our witnesses and your prepared statements, without objection, will be made a part of the record. And members may have 5 days to insert statements and questions for the record, subject to the length limitation in the rules.

And the Chair now recognizes herself for 5 minutes.

Egypt has always been of central importance to the Middle East and the region's stability. It has also been a strategic interest for the United States, our policy objectives in the region, and our national security. The Suez Canal remains an all-important waterway that serves as a strategic asset for global trade and, just as importantly, the avenue which U.S. warships can easily traverse between the Mediterranean and the Persian Gulf.

Over the past 4 years, we have certainly seen Egypt undergo drastic changes. As policymakers, we face one of the more difficult challenges in Egypt, and today's hearing is entitled Egypt: Two Years After Morsi, to examine the ever-changing dynamics on the ground of that country.

Since the 2011 revolution, the change we had hoped to see for Egypt has been slow to come, to say the least. For many of us, myself included, we believe that human rights is a top priority that must be taken into account as we formulate our foreign policy objective. We want to see people living in free democratic and open societies where everyone can practice, without fear, their religion and where everyone is treated equally and fairly.

In March of this year, an Egyptian court ruled that parliamentary elections had to be postponed, marking a major setback in Egypt's path to democracy. The authorities in Egypt and different branches of government must work together to ensure that the elections are scheduled as quickly as possible and in accordance with Egyptian law.

It is important to note that elections for the sake of elections are not the only requirement for a democracy. A government must also govern democratically and respect the rights of its citizens. But we also understand that there can be no economic prosperity and no political stability without safety and security. And right now Egypt faces threats from the Sinai and along its border with Libya, and Cairo plays an important role as a counterbalance to the Iranian regime's hegemonic ambitions in the region.

Egypt has taken a very active role in the Sinai, which for years has been ignored by Cairo, and is confronting the radical terror groups, some affiliated with ISIL. Egypt has long been a vital— Egypt has also been vital in cutting off and destroying the tunnels in Gaza used by Hamas and has been working closely with Israel to combat their shared threats.

Earlier this year, the administration decided to resume weapons transfers to Egypt to help Cairo counter some of these threats. In 2013, Mr. Connolly and I commissioned a three-phase report from the Government Accountability Office to assess our foreign assistance to Egypt. The GAO is currently conducting this third phase, which will assess the security-related assistance, and the timing could not be more important as we resume these weapons sales.

It is in our national security interest to see that these terror threats are eliminated and that Egypt remains a strategic ally and continues to have a good working relationship with Israel.

Recently, Egypt has taken moves that signal that it is willing to move away from the U.S. toward a closer relationship with Russia. Russia has agreed to build a nuclear powerplant in Egypt, and the two have increased trade dramatically over the past year, and Putin has vowed to increase Russian weapons sales to Egypt.

We cannot afford to allow Putin to undermine our ties with Egypt. It would be a serious blow to our national security interests. But as friends, it is also important that we take issue with Cairo's lack of progress on the domestic front. I still remain deeply concerned over the fate of 43 NGO workers, many of whom are American citizens who were convicted in absentia in a sham politically motivated trial.

It would be a simple but important gesture for Sisi to pardon these individuals and signal that he is willing to move Egypt forward in a positive direction and could improve the U.S.-Egypt bilateral relationship.

We should also look to reexamine the controversial laws against civil society, like the NGO law and the protest law. As much as the Egyptian people appreciate safety, security, and economic growth after the recent instability, they are also seeking far-reaching changes to the political process and the people's relationship with the state.

President Sisi should seize this opportunity to move forward on long-needed democratic reforms, and the U.S. can play an important role in that effort. What it boils down to is finding the right balance between security and democracy, and the United States must ensure that we leverage our assistance to promote both simultaneously.

With that, I am pleased to yield to the ranking member of our subcommittee, Mr. Deutch.

Mr. DEUTCH. Thank you, Madam Chairman. This hearing was intended to give members of this subcommittee the opportunity to take a broad look at the issues affecting Egypt today and the U.S.-Egypt relationship.

I would like to take a moment to thank the chairman and my colleague, Mr. Connolly, who have been extremely focused on bringing justice to those 43 NGO workers who have still not been pardoned, including our witness here today, Dr. Okail. We must continue to press for this justice.

Since the overthrow of Mubarak, there have been differing opinions on Capitol Hill as to how we should approach Egypt. But I think we all agree that Egypt plays a critical role in a very volatile region, and it is, and should continue to be, an important partner of the United States.

We want to see Egypt succeed economically, and we want to see long-term stability and safety. In 2011, the people of Egypt bravely took to the streets to seek freedoms and rights long denied under the autocratic rule of Mubarak. We were under no illusions then that this transition would be easy. We could not then, and we cannot now, expect Egyptian democracy to look like ours overnight.

The subsequent election of Mohamed Morsi in 2012 was significant, but it was Morsi's government who chose to jam through a new constitution with exceptional executive authority. It was Morsi's government that failed to make tough economic choices, like reducing government subsidies to meet IMF requirements that would put the country back on a path to prosperity. And it was Morsi's government who restricted the political space, cutting out those who sought to bring real democratic values to Egypt.

So, in the summer of 2013, the people of Egypt again took to the streets to protest the barely year-old government, setting in motion the rise of the well-known military commander General al-Sisi. After another year of transition and interim government, the country held a second presidential election in 2 years, electing the long respected general.

For many, the election of President Sisi represented a return to normalcy. The Sisi government seemed to understand the need to return economic investment to Egypt and to strengthen the country's regional ties. The Gulf States infused Egypt with billions of dollars, with hopes of cementing the new government as a stabilizing force.

A recent IMF review found that the Egyptian economy has begun to grow, and I was pleased to see the successful results of the economic investment confidence in March, which yielded some $60 billion in investment pledges. I urge the government to continue to take the tough steps needed to restore Egypt's financial stability and to bring relief to the people.

Many of us here in Washington have also welcomed President Sisi's commitment to security issues. The government has faced a daunting challenge of policing the Sinai, which had become virtually lawless in the years after Mubarak. President Sisi made clear that he would continue close cooperation with Israel's military to prevent terror groups from exploiting this region. These efforts have come at great cost to the Egyptian military, and we are grateful for them.

President Sisi has been committed to stopping Hamas from building and using terror tunnels to smuggle weapons into Gaza. The government has destroyed hundreds of tunnels, and in a speech last week President Sisi estimated his forces have destroyed 80 percent of these tunnels.

Egypt is also facing great challenges on its borders with Sudan and Libya, as these countries become havens for terror training and weapons transit. We all mourn the victims of the gruesome attack on Egyptian Christians by ISIS affiliates in Libya, and I, too, am greatly concerned about Libya's potential to descend into greater chaos, but military action could potentially provoke even greater internal instability.

Nevertheless, I agree with our Egyptian partners that the international community must play a role in getting Libya back on track, and I appreciate Egypt's close cooperation with its neighbors as they seek to address regional threats as a regional bloc. I believe the United States must continue to support Egypt, and I support continued assistance.

But I am pleased to see our administration moving forward with a rebalance of our aid relationship that will allow Egypt to better address the most pressing threats and continue to cooperate with the U.S. in significant areas like counterterrorism. But like many friends of Egypt, I am concerned about the erosion of civil society and human rights in the name of security.

Regardless of who sits in power, the United States should be delivering the same message to every government leader. And the message is clear: Human rights matter. I am concerned that too many restrictions have been placed on free expression. I am concerned about the arrests of journalists and about religious freedom, and I am concerned about laws that restrict the work of civil society actors or prevent any form of peaceful assembly.

There must be a way to balance necessary security measures while protecting and enhancing the basic freedoms of the people of Egypt. This includes fostering good governance, rule of law, and routing out corruption and accountability for security services and government actors. And I have to say I was particularly dismayed this week to see media reports of rampant sexual abuse by policy and security services.

I am also concerned about the impact of mass arrests and the handing down of mass death sentences. I hope our witnesses can speak to the message that this sends to society.

And I also hope to hear from our witnesses their thoughts on the death sentence handed down on Monday to Morsi and how it has been received by the Egyptian people. As I have said, I believe in a strong Egypt and a strong U.S.-Egypt partnership. I want to see Egypt move forward on a path to stability and democracy, but even the closest of friends must be able to share and work through concerns.

Today, I look to our witnesses to help us understand how we can balance and strengthen this relationship and ensure a successful future for all of the people of Egypt. And I yield back.

Thank you, Madam Chair.

Ms. Ros-Lehtinen. Thank you very much, Mr. Deutch.

I am now pleased to yield to other members for their opening statements. Mr. Rohrabacher of California.

Mr. ROHRABACHER. Thank you very much for holding this hearing today. What happens in Egypt will determine the future not only of the Middle East but of the world, and we need to understand that. If Egypt falls under the control of the radical Islamic forces that now threaten that region, what we will have is the Gulf countries one by one will fall like leaves from a tree as the whole dynamic of that region will change.

Radical Islam will then thrust itself into Central Asia, and within a short time we will have a monstrous threat to Western civilization, a historic change, C change, that could for many years turn—put us into a situation of danger and a dark future. There is only person and one regime and one government that stands in the way of that, and that is President al-Sisi of Egypt. We owe him and the people of Egypt our utmost support to prevent this horrible scenario for the rest of the world and the rest of that region.

Thank you very much, Madam Chairman.

Ms. ROS-LEHTINEN. Thank you, Mr. Rohrabacher.

Mr. Connolly.

Mr. CONNOLLY. Thank you, Madam Chairman. Timely hearing and glad we were able to collaborate on a report in terms of the status of U.S. aid. The fact of the matter is, a coup occurred in Egypt, and the United States Government has yet formally to acknowledge that because of the consequences under the law.

The military alliance with Egypt is a very important one, and I understand putting a certain primacy on that, but we have paid a price for it. So have the Egyptian people, with respect to rule of law, with respect to civic engagement, with respect to the need to create political space.

As the current Egyptian government moves forward, hopefully we can make progress in all of these areas. If we don't, the crackdown that has occurred is going to lead to a backlash that will lead us we don't know where, but certainly we won't like it, and it probably will have consequences far beyond the current consequences of the military government.

So I am looking forward to hearing the testimony today and where we are in terms of these areas with the current Egyptian government.

Thank you, Madam Chairman.

Ms. ROS-LEHTINEN. Thank you, sir.

Mr. Meadows.

Mr. MEADOWS. Thank you, Madam Chairman. Thank you each for your testimony here today. We look forward to hearing it. I apologize, I am going to have to step out, back and forth, but we are monitoring this. I think it is critical that we are here today making great progress.

Ambassador Tawfik is a good friend here, and I consider him a personal friend. In both the good and the bad times we have talked about the progress that is being made in Egypt. It is imperative that the American people know that we stand by the Egyptians wanting to govern Egypt, and it is not America wanting to impose its values on Egypt, but it is also critical that Egypt stands so strong in a very tough neighborhood to really add that stability.

6

And so I look forward to hearing your testimony, look forward to working with the Egyptian people in bringing not only the rule of law back front and center but certainly investments from the United States to continue to flow back to Egypt.

Thank you, Madam Chair. I yield back.

Ms. ROS-LEHTINEN. Thank you very much, Mr. Meadows.

Mr. Cicilline.

Mr CICILLINE. Thank you, Chairman and Ranking Member, for calling this very timely hearing on Egypt after Morsi. And thank you to our witnesses for being here today.

My view is that the post-Morsi description only gets at part of the equation in Egypt. The Egyptian people have experienced an incredible amount of disruption, chaos, and change over the past 4 years. They are living in a post-Mubarak, post-Revolutionary, and post-Morsi era. And today they are living under a regime that is perhaps most aptly described as Mubarak 2.0, turning to oppression in the name of security.

However, there are some significant differences between the landscape now and Egypt under Mubarak. Waves of unrest have left the Middle East in utter chaos, have increased terrorist attacks and flow of refugees in Egypt. The United States has watched as two successive governments were toppled and is now reevaluating some of its longstanding policies toward the Egyptian government.

But most importantly the Egyptian people have seen what they can do. They have experienced what they can achieve when they stand together in support of human rights and democratic freedoms against a tyrannical regime. And I think the question we need to ask is whether the Egyptian people who have won and lost so much over the past 4 years are willing to live under a regime that resorts to the same old tactics of intimidation, repression, and violence against their own people in the name of security.

I think ultimately they are not, and that our policies toward Egypt need to reflect not just a security relationship, which is vitally important, but also the reality that the model of supporting an autocratic regime is inherently unstable in the long term.

We absolutely must push the al-Sisi regime to enact democratic reforms and respectful fundamental human rights, and I fear that Egypt will find itself once again in the midst of volatile leadership change if we do not.

Thank you to the witnesses for being here today, and I look forward to your testimony.

Ms. ROS-LEHTINEN. Thank you, Mr. Cicilline.

Mr. Trott.

Mr. TROTT. I want to thank the chairwoman and Ranking Member for holding this timely and critical hearing. And to the witnesses, thank you for taking your time to share your insight on the state of Egypt.

I am from southeast Michigan, and I am proud to represent a large and vibrant Coptic community. It is a church with a long history, but it often seems that their interests and concerns since the 2011 uprising have gone unnoticed, if not completely ignored. While the Copts have been largely in peril since St. Mark brought Christianity to Egypt over 2,000 years ago, the 2011 revolution brought renewed hopes of freedom, tolerance, and more prominent participation in public life.

As we have seen through various governments that have each had control over Egypt since Mubarak's downfall, the Copts continue to be marginalized or used as a political tool. Sectarian conflicts in rural areas often lead to government-controlled reconciliation sessions, which tend to leave the victims with no justice and the defendant with no more than a slap on the wrist.

Under Morsi's regime, the Copts were subject to blatant sectarian rhetoric, inaction by state security, and even an attack by state security forces on the Coptic Cathedral. Subsequently, after Morsi's overthrow, there was what only can be described as unprecedented coordinated attacks on numerous Coptic Christian institutions. In what could only be viewed as a series of positive developments, President Sisi promised to repair and rebuild numerous Coptic churches and recently called for a religious revolution.

Today, I look forward to hearing from my colleagues and the esteemed witnesses on how the Copts are faring under President Sisi and the current state of U.S.-Egypt relations.

Thank you for your time today.

Ms. Ros-Lehtinen. Excellent statements from all members, and now we would like to introduce our panelists.

First, we welcome Dr. Eric Trager, who is currently the Esther K. Wagner fellow at The Washington Institute for Near East Policy. Dr. Trager is an expert on Egyptian politics and has taught at the University of Michigan—Go Blue—and at the University of Pennsylvania.

Welcome, Dr. Trager.

Second, we welcome Mr. Samuel Tadros, who is a senior fellow at the Hudson Institute's Center for Religious Freedom. Previously, he was a senior partner at the Egyptian Union of Liberal Youth and a lecturer at the School of Advanced International Studies at Johns Hopkins University.

Welcome.

And last, but certainly not least, we welcome Dr. Nancy Okail. Dr. Okail is the executive director of the Tahrir Institute for Middle East Policy and has 12 years' experience promoting democracy and development in the Middle East and North Africa. And, as we have heard, she is quite active in promoting peace and democracy in Egypt.

Prior to joining the Tahrir Institute, she served as the director of the Egypt program at Freedom House and is one of the 43 defendants convicted and sentenced to prison in the political trial of the NGO workers in Egypt.

So we welcome you as well, Doctor.

And we will begin with you, Dr. Trager.

STATEMENT OF ERIC TRAGER, PH.D., ESTHER K. WAGNER FELLOW, THE WASHINGTON INSTITUTE FOR NEAR EAST POLICY

Mr. Trager. Madam Chair, Ranking Member Deutch, it is a privilege to be here again before this subcommittee and to sit on this very distinguished panel.

Nearly 2 years ago, on June 30, 2013, unprecedented millions of protestors turned out across Egypt to demand President Mohamed Morsi's ouster. While Morsi, a Muslim Brotherhood leader, narrowly won the June 2012 presidential elections, he rapidly lost support. Morsi's assertion of total power through a November 2012 edict alienated a substantial cross-section of the Egyptian public, igniting demonstrations that continued for months.

Then, as the economy plummeted and the tide of popular opinion shifted further against Morsi, Egypt's state institutions mutinied. As a result, the Egyptian state was on the brink of collapse. Meanwhile, rather than offering a political compromise, the Muslim Brotherhood mobilized thousands of its cadres to defend Morsi's presidency, and indicated that it would use violence if necessary.

This is the context in which Egypt's military, led by then Defense Minister Abdul Fattah al-Sisi removed Morsi from power. Egypt was on the verge of severe civil strife, if not civil war, and many Egyptians feared that their country was headed the way of Syria or Libya, yet the manner of Morsi's ouster had significant consequences for Egypt's democratic prospects. By toppling Morsi, the Egyptian military locked itself in a "kill or be killed" struggle with the Brotherhood.

The generals believe that they must destroy the Brotherhood or risk the Brotherhood remobilizing and seeking vengeance. And this fear is hardly theoretical; the Brotherhood openly calls for President Sisi's death; and it released a statement in January calling for jihad and martyrdom in fighting the regime.

As a result, the post-Morsi period is perhaps the most brutal in Egypt's contemporary history. Over 2,500 people have been killed, and over 16,000 have been detained. These developments are quite dispiriting for those who hope that the Arab Springs represented the dawn of a more democratic era in the Arab world.

But at the same time, Washington should be realistic. It cannot influence Egypt in a more democratic direction, so long as the government and the Muslim Brotherhood are locked in an existential struggle with each other.

To be sure, the administration has tried to influence Egypt's political trajectory. In October 2013, the administration withheld most of the $1.3 billion in annual military aid to Egypt "pending credible progress toward an inclusive, democratically elected civilian government." This was a lose-lose proposition. Withholding military aid had no impact on Egypt's authoritarianism. And at the same time, it soured the strategic relationship between Washington and Cairo in ways that have been mentioned earlier today.

For this reason, the administration reversed its policy in March and resumed the aid. It is not in Washington's interest to have tense relations with Cairo. After all, Egypt is an important strategic partner. It coordinates with Washington a wide range of regional activities and has maintained a peace treaty with Israel since 1979. Washington relies on Egypt to grant preferred access to the Suez Canal and overflight rights to equip U.S. military bases in the Persian Gulf, and to support the current efforts against ISIS.

President Sisi is also far more aligned with U.S. interest than Morsi. First, Egypt is once again a strategic partner against Iran. Whereas Morsi was the first Egyptian President to visit Tehran since 1979, President Sisi has deployed the Egyptian Navy against the Iranian-backed Houthis in Yemen and expelled the Iranian Ambassador.

As the administration seeks a nuclear arrangement with Iran, strengthening the U.S.-Egypt relationship can help reassure Washington's allies in the Persian Gulf.

Second, Egypt is now aggressively battling jihadists in the Sinai. After refusing to act for many years, the Egyptian military launched a major operation in September 2013 against the jihadists, some of whom now affiliate with ISIS.

Third, Egypt's relationship with Israel has never been stronger. Whereas, Morsi refused to establish a channel between his presidential office and the Israeli government, President Sisi communicates openly and directly with his Israeli counterpart. There is also unprecedented Egyptian-Israeli coordination on the Sinai.

Fourth, Egypt is now constraining rather than aiding Hamas, which is a U.S. designated terrorist organization. Indeed, whereas Morsi welcomed Hamas officials to the Presidential Palace in Cairo, the Sisi government has shut down Hamas' Cairo suburban headquarters.

In closing, the proper policy toward Egypt is for Washington to cooperate with Cairo on regional strategy but not condone its repressiveness. If Washington doesn't draw this distinction, if it instead conditions its relationship with Cairo on its progress toward democracy, the strategic relationship will suffer without any positive impact on Egypt's domestic politics.

Thank you for listening.

[The prepared statement of Mr. Trager follows:]

Egypt Two Years After Morsi: Part I

Eric Trager
Esther K. Wagner Fellow,
The Washington Institute for Near East Policy

Testimony submitted to the House Committee on Foreign Affairs
May 20, 2015

Madam Chair, Ranking Member Deutch, it is a privilege to be here again before this subcommittee, particularly to discuss a subject of such great importance to American interests and security as the U.S.-Egypt relationship.

Nearly two years ago, on June 30, 2013, unprecedented millions of protestors descended on the central squares across Egypt to demand President Mohamed Morsi's ouster. While Morsi, a Muslim Brotherhood leader, had narrowly won the June 2012 presidential elections, he rapidly lost support. Morsi's assertion of total executive power through a November 2012 constitutional declaration alienated a substantial cross section of the Egyptian public, setting off frequent -- and often violent -- demonstrations that continued for months. Meanwhile, as the economy plummeted and the tide of popular opinion shifted further against Morsi, Egypt's state institutions mutinied: bureaucracies became unresponsive to Brotherhood ministers, police refused to guard Brotherhood properties, and in some cases uniformed officers even stood alongside anti-Morsi protestors in the streets. As a result, the Egyptian state was on the brink of collapse: by the time the massive June 30, 2013, demonstrations began, Morsi controlled practically nothing on the ground, and he was reduced to being a president in name only.

The Muslim Brotherhood, however, utterly misinterpreted the depth of this crisis, and refused to negotiate a political solution, such as early elections or a referendum on Morsi's presidency. Instead, it mobilized thousands of its cadres to defend Morsi's "legitimacy," and indicated that it would use violence if necessary. At the Brotherhood's protest site in northern Cairo's Rabaa al-Adawiya Square, I personally witnessed hundreds of Muslim Brothers marching in formation as a vigilante group, chanting threatening slogans. Meanwhile, clashes between Muslim Brothers and their opponents erupted throughout the country, in which dozens were killed.

This is the context in which Egypt's military, led by then defense minister Abdul Fattah al-Sisi, removed Morsi from power on July 3, 2013. Egypt was on the verge of severe civil strife, if not civil war, and many Egyptians feared that their country was headed the way of Syria or Libya. Indeed, from the perspective of the generals and many Egyptians, Sisi's decision to oust Morsi saved Egypt from outright chaos.

Yet the manner in which Morsi was removed from power had significant consequences for Egypt's democratic prospects. By toppling Morsi, the Egyptian military locked itself in a kill-or-be-killed struggle with the Brotherhood. The generals and their supporters believe that they must destroy the Brotherhood, or risk the

Brotherhood remobilizing, returning to power, and seeking vengeance for Morsi's overthrow. And by the same token, the Brotherhood seeks to destroy the current government. In this vein, Brotherhood leaders openly call for Sisi's death, and the Brotherhood released a statement in January 2015 calling on its followers to embrace "jihad" and "martyrdom" in fighting the current regime. So after removing Morsi, Egypt's military-backed government launched a brutal crackdown on the Brotherhood, repressing its protests with deadly force while decapitating the Brotherhood's hierarchical command-chain through a massive arrest campaign. This past weekend's death sentences for dozens of Brotherhood figures, including Morsi, constitute merely the latest chapter in the brutal power struggle that has defined Egypt's domestic politics in the post-Morsi period.

The repression, however, has not stopped at the Brotherhood. Because the current regime sees most opposition activity as possibly enabling the Brotherhood's return, it has also cracked down on media criticism, non-Islamist opposition activism, and youth protests. And because many Egyptians are weary of political tumult and frightened by an upsurge of terrorist attacks within Egypt's major cities, they are largely supportive of this crackdown -- and, in many cases, encourage Egypt's police to deal with the Brotherhood and other oppositionists even more forcefully.

Of course, these dynamics are quite dispiriting for those who hoped that the 2011 Arab Spring uprisings represented the dawn of a more democratic era in the Arab world, with Egypt leading the way. And Washington should in no way downplay the current Egyptian government's repressiveness, such as by declaring that Cairo is "transitioning toward democracy," as Secretary of State John Kerry did in July 2014. But Washington should be realistic about its ability to influence Egypt in a more democratic direction so long as the government and the Muslim Brotherhood remain in a life-and-death struggle with each other.

To be sure, the Obama administration has tried. In October 2013, the administration withheld most of the $1.3 billion in annual military aid to Egypt "pending credible progress toward an inclusive, democratically elected civilian government." This was a lose-lose proposition: withholding military aid had no impact on Egypt's domestic politics, which remained quite autocratic, and at the same time it soured the strategic relationship between Washington and Cairo. In lieu of the U.S.-made F-16 fighter jets that are part of Egypt's military aid package, Egypt inked a $5.4 billion weapons deal with France. It also signed a preliminary $3.5 billion weapons deal with Russia, and granted Russian president Vladimir Putin a hero's welcome when he visited Cairo in February 2015. Meanwhile, Egypt reportedly partnered with the United Arab Emirates to attack jihadist sites in Libya without coordinating with Washington, and similarly rejected U.S. assistance in Sinai.

The Obama administration effectively recognized its blunder seventeen months later, in March 2015, when it announced that it would resume the $1.3 billion in aid to Egypt. But to signal its ongoing displeasure with Egypt's domestic political trajectory, it announced the end of cash-flow financing of aid to Egypt after 2017. As a result, the U.S.-Egypt relationship will likely remain tense: if Cairo cannot depend on the reliable flow of aid that cash-flow financing entails, it will likely continue turning to other partners for weapons, including partners that do not necessarily share U.S. interests in the Middle East.

Fueling this tension isn't in Washington's interests, given Egypt's role as an important U.S. strategic partner. Egypt has maintained a peace treaty with Israel since 1979, and coordinates with Washington on a wide range of regional activities, including counterterrorism and diplomacy. Washington further relies on Egypt to grant preferred access in the Suez Canal and overflight rights to equip U.S. military bases in the Persian Gulf, and to support the current efforts against the Islamic State of Iraq and al-Sham (ISIS).

But perhaps more to the point, the Sisi government represents a major opportunity for Washington, because it is significantly more closely aligned with U.S. interests than the Brotherhood-dominated government that preceded it. Consider the following:

- **Egypt is once again a strategic partner against Iran.** Following former president Hosni Mubarak's ouster in February 2011, the ruling Supreme Council of the Armed Forces (SCAF) reversed more than three decades of tense relations with Iran by permitting Iranian warships to transit the Suez Canal. Egypt-Iran relations warmed further under Morsi. His August 2012 visit to Tehran marked the first visit by an Egyptian leader since 1979, and Morsi hosted then Iranian president Mahmoud Ahmadinejad in Cairo in February 2013. The Brotherhood viewed its engagement with Iran as a mechanism for moving away from Washington's orbit and having more "balanced" global relations. Under Sisi, however, Egypt has returned to its prior anti-Iran posture: it has deployed its navy to prevent the Iran-backed Houthis from disrupting maritime traffic in the Bab al-Mandab Strait, and recently expelled the Iranian ambassador from Cairo on account of Iran's aggressive regional activities. So as the Obama administration seeks a nuclear arrangement with Iran, strengthening the U.S.-Egypt relationship can help reassure Washington's Sunni Arab allies in the Persian Gulf that the United States isn't pivoting toward Tehran.

- **Egypt is, for the first time in its history, aggressively battling jihadists in the Sinai.** For many years, the Egyptian government rebuffed Washington's calls to confront jihadists in the Sinai Peninsula. The Egyptian military did not want to be held responsible for operations that, in its view, were the purview of intelligence and the Ministry of Interior. And during his year in power, Morsi similarly refused to authorize an aggressive campaign against the jihadists, since the Brotherhood believed that its electoral success would convince the jihadists to lay down their arms and embrace the Brotherhood's approach of "implementing sharia" through the ballot box. As a result, the jihadist threat grew significantly, and exploded in the months that followed Morsi's ouster, during which hundreds of Egyptian security personnel were killed. Since September 2013, however, the Egyptian military has been actively fighting the Sinai jihadists, some of whom have declared their loyalty to ISIS. The Egyptian military has also aggressively targeted the tunnel network that links Sinai and Gaza, which the jihadists used for escaping Sinai to hide and receive medical treatment.

- **Egypt's relationship with Israel has never been stronger.** Despite being president of a country that signed a peace treaty with Israel in 1979, Morsi refused to establish a communication channel between his presidential office and the Israeli government. Meanwhile, the Muslim Brotherhood repeatedly signaled that it intended to alter or end the peace treaty, such as by holding a popular referendum or parliamentary vote on it. By contrast, President Sisi communicates directly with Israeli prime minister Binyamin Netanyahu -- and openly acknowledges this fact. The Sisi era has also witnessed unprecedented coordination between Israel and Egypt on counterterrorism in the Sinai.

- **Egypt is constraining, rather than aiding, Hamas.** Hamas is the Palestinian branch of the Muslim Brotherhood, and Morsi's victory in the June 2012 elections benefited it considerably. Morsi became the first Egyptian president to welcome Hamas officials to the presidential palace in Cairo, thereby affording Hamas the same diplomatic treatment as the Palestinian Authority receives. Morsi's ouster, however, reversed Hamas's fortunes: Hamas leaders' diplomatic access in Cairo diminished and its office in a Cairo suburb was shut down. Meanwhile, the Egyptian military has taken unprecedented measures to close the tunnels that are used to smuggle goods, weapons, and personnel from Sinai into Gaza.

To be sure, the Obama administration is right to be concerned about Egypt's domestic political trajectory, and it should use its diplomatic engagement with the Sisi government to encourage greater tolerance and political pluralism. But if Washington conditions its strategic relationship with Cairo on Egypt's progress toward democracy, it won't achieve democracy in Egypt given the current circumstances, and will hurt the bilateral strategic relationship in the process.

The current regional environment makes it particularly urgent for Washington to restore its relationship with Egypt on the basis of shared strategic interests. Specifically, Congress should encourage the Obama administration to proceed with the "strategic dialogue" that Cairo has requested since early 2014. This is an important opportunity to review the military aid relationship in a bilateral setting, and to coordinate both countries' strategies on a wide range of regional challenges.

Ms. ROS-LEHTINEN. Thank you so much.

Mr. Tadros.

STATEMENT OF MR. SAMUEL TADROS, SENIOR FELLOW, HUDSON INSTITUTE

Mr. TADROS. Madam Chairman, Ranking Member Deutch, distinguished members of the committee, thank you for holding this important hearing and for inviting me to testify today.

For the past 4½ years, and after decades of political stagnation, the foundations of the political order in Egypt were shaken to their core as the country's citizens struggled with questions of democracy, the rule of law, and the country's identity.

In June 2013, following popular protests, the military removed President Morsi from power, promising the Egyptian people not only to bring about stability and security but also equal citizenship and prosperity. Those hopes are today on the shoulder of President Sisi following his elections.

While Egypt faces numerous challenges—security, economic, and political—I will limit—or I will focus in my testimony on religious freedom questions on the rule of law. I would be happy to address other aspects of Egypt's challenges in the Q&A.

On the 26 of March 2015, a mob gathered in the village of El Galaa in Minya governorate and began attacking Christian homes and shops. The mob was incensed that Christians had received a permit to build a church in the village. Instead of protecting the Christians from that attack, the security forces allowed the attack to take place and, after the attack was concluded, held a reconciliation session between the elders of both communities to see how the situation can be calmed.

The result was a number of demands by the mob. The church that was to be built would have no dome, no cross, no tower, no bell, and its entrance was to be on a side street, i.e. it should have no outer manifestation of Christianity. The security forces forced Copts to accept those demands in order for the church to be built, despite Copts having the necessary permits for their church.

The mob then continued its attack, demanding further that the Copts who had spread news of the attack in the local and international press would publish an apology for those attacking them for tarnishing the image of the village Muslim residents. Again, those attacks went unpunished, with the regime arresting an equal number from those attacked and attacking in order to hold the reconciliation session, again to force reconciliation between them without implementation of the rule of law.

Until today this church has not been built. This is unfortunately not an isolated incident. Similar incidents have taken place in the village of Al Our, which represents where 13 of those Copts that were beheaded by ISIS in Libya come from. While President Sisi promised to build a church in that village, after protests by the residents in that village the location of that church was to be moved to the outskirts of the village instead of inside.

Similarly, we have seen the continuation of blasphemy accusations and trials under President Sisi. Those have included a number of Christians, Shiites that have been arrested for simply praying, or for the possession of Shiite books. That is considered a crime that has led to 6 months for a Shiite person in prison.

Similarly, atheists have received sentences from 1 to 3 years for simply posting their views and their beliefs on Facebook. Despite the Egyptian government undertaking a number of symbolic steps toward religious freedom, including President Sisi's call for a religious revolution, and his visit to the Coptic Cathedral, it has failed to implement the rule of law, protect the country's most vulnerable citizens from those attacks taking place.

The basis of the Egyptian-American relationship has been, since 1974 following former Secretary of State Henry Kissinger's visit, that Egypt would become a regional player in the sight of the United States, that it would play a leading role in the peace process, in leading the whole region to peace with Israel, and to stability and prosperity.

For the past 30 years, that relationship has held. Egypt, despite disagreements with the United States, plays an important role in the peace process, in the defeat of Saddam's invasion of Kuwait, and in a host of other issues. Yet the Egypt of today is no longer the Egypt of the past. Egypt is no longer a regional player that can lead the region to anything, but instead is a play field itself, with a host of international, local, and regional powers competing for the country's future trajectory.

The United States needs to base its relationship with Egypt not on the dreams of an Egypt that no longer exists, but instead on the reality that no one wants an Egypt that looks like Somalia, no one wants a Somalia on the Nile, no one wants a Libya bordering Israel, and no one wants a Syria in control of the Suez Canal.

Thank you.

[The prepared statement of Mr. Tadros follows:]

House Committee on Foreign Affairs
Subcommittee on the Middle East and North Africa

Egypt Two Years After Morsi: Part 1

Testimony of Samuel Tadros
Senior Fellow, Hudson Institute's Center for Religious
Freedom
20 May 2015

Madam Chairman, Ranking member Deutch, distinguished members of the committee, thank you for holding this important hearing and for inviting me to testify today on Egypt two years after Morsi.

For the past four and a half years and after decades of political stagnation, the foundations of the political order in Egypt were shaken to their core as the country's citizens struggled with questions of democracy, the rule of law, and the country's identity. In July 2013, following popular protests, the military removed President Morsi from office and promised the Egyptian people not only a new era of stability and security, but also of equal citizenship and prosperity. Following his election to the Egyptian presidency in May 2014, the task of implementing those dreams lies with President Sisi. While Egypt faces enormous political, security and economic challenges, the focus of my testimony today will be on the questions of religious freedom, the rule of law and calls for religious reform. I would be happy to address other aspects of Egypt's challenges in the Q&A session.

On the 26th of March 2015, a mob gathered in the village of El Galaa in Minya governorate and began attacking Christian homes and shops. The mob was incensed that Christians had received a permit to demolish and rebuild their local church, which served 1.400 Copts. With their old church building decaying and their numbers growing, Copts had received a permit in 2004 to build a new larger church, but were continuously prevented from doing so. In January 2015 they sought to avoid a confrontation by attempting to renovate the old one, only to get attacked by the mob. In what has become a recurring practice, the mob demanded that the church would have no outer symbol of Christianity: no dome, no cross, no tower, no bell, and that its entrance be on a side street. Instead of protecting the Copts and upholding the rule of law by allowing the church to be built, the security forces and local authorities forced Copts into a reconciliation session and pressured them to accept the mob's demands. Encouraged by the police's conduct, the mob added a new demand. Copts were to publish an apology in newspapers to local Muslims for complaining informing the media of the attack and thus tarnishing the village's image. Furthermore, Copts were to sign an agreement never to seek to build a new church if the old one was damaged in the future. After Copts refused to accept those demands, the attack was renewed on the 4th of April with rocks thrown at Christian homes and Christian shops were looted. Seven Copts were wound in the attack. In typical fashion, security forces arrested 28 men from the village including 12 Copts. Such practices are intended to pressure Copts to agree to a new reconciliation session. To date, Copts have been prevented from building their church.

Unfortunately this episode in El Galaa village is hardly unique. In the neighboring Al Our village, home to 13 of the Copts beheaded in Libya by ISIS, a mob attacked Coptic homes on the 27th of March in order to similarly prevent a church from being built. That construction of that church had been ordered by President Sisi to honor the Coptic martyrs and as a symbol of a new Egypt where Copts were to be treated as equal citizens. Instead the church became a symbol of an Egypt in which Copts suffer from violence because of their faith and are treated as second class citizens. The mob attack involved rocks and Molotov cocktails. Rather than upholding the rule of law by arresting and prosecuting the attackers, the governor organized a reconciliation session between both communities. Unable to walk back the President's promise, the local authorities forced Copts to accept that the proposed church be banished to the village outskirts. The authorities' actions naturally encouraged the mob further and on the 29th of April, the house of one of the ISIS victims in Libya was attacked.

Similar incidents have taken place in the village of Taleyhat in Sohag governorate on the 11th of April, where the mob was angered by rumors of the church acquiring a dome. The mob was not alone however in attacking Copts. On the 9th of April, security forces prevented Copts from building a church in Abu Qurqas, Minya governorate. On April 4th, security forces attacked a building used by Copts as a church for over a decade in Maghagha confiscating altar equipment and bibles. Bishop Aghathon, in whose diocese the church is located, has publically accused security forces of inciting local Muslims against their Christian neighbors.

Threats to religious freedom are however not limited to violent attacks. Religious minorities such as Copts, Baha'is, and Shias have suffered from a host of official discriminatory policies for decades. These include tremendous restrictions on the building and renovation of churches, exclusion of Christians from key government positions, punishment of converts to Christianity, arrests of Shi'a for practicing their faith, and not refusing to issue government identification cards to Baha'is. While the level of discrimination and persecution has varied under successive regimes, it has been a part of a continued and increasing pattern.

Following the Egyptian revolution of 2011, a new threat emerged in the form of blasphemy accusations with subsequent verdicts in cases that have ranged from the accused posting something on Facebook deemed offensive to Islam to simply being tagged in such a post. Such accusations are automatically accompanied by attacks by the local mob on, not only the accused's house, but all surrounding Christian homes. Subsequent trials have been a mockery of justice with courts in some cases surrounded by an angry mob and the accused denied legal representation.

Under President Sisi, blasphemy accusations and trials have continued. On January 10, Karim Ashraf El Banna was sentenced for three years in prison. The Appeals Court has subsequently upheld his conviction. On February 16, Sherif Gaber received a one year sentence for creating an atheist Facebook page. On April 28, Michael Mounir Bishay was sentenced to one year in prison for sharing a video, which had aired on an Egyptian TV channel on Facebook. On May 12, Shia Mahmoud Dahroug received a six months sentence for possessing Shia books at his home. Lastly on April 8th, a Coptic teacher and five Coptic students were arrested for filming a video making fun of ISIS. No verdict has been issued yet in their case.

The above mentioned attacks and blasphemy cases are hardly the first and will unfortunately not be the last unless the Egyptian regime begins to seriously address the root causes of Egypt's endemic sectarian crisis. Failure by the Sisi regime to uphold the rule of law and protect the country's Christians from attack bodes ill for the Middle East's largest Christian community. While the Egyptian regime believes that its resort to reconciliation sessions instead of punishing the attackers helps in restoring and maintaining order, the reality is the exact opposite. The lack of punishment has created a culture of impunity, which in turn has become a culture of encouragement. Fanatics have rightly concluded that attacking Copts, not only will go unpunished, but more importantly will result in the mob's demands being met. The Egyptian regime needs to offer better protection of its most vulnerable citizens preventing the attacks from taking place, and enforce the rule of law by bringing attackers to justice. The Egyptian regime needs to understand that protecting religious minorities is not a luxurious act to be done after serious security threats are dealt with or that punishing those attacking them can wait until stability and security is restored. Those attacking Copts share the same hatreds that fuels the terrorists and no stability or security can be achieved if criminals are not punished. Likewise, blasphemy accusations should not be used as a means to terrorize religious minorities.

President Sisi has undertaken some symbolic gestures towards Copts such as visiting the Coptic Cathedral on Christmas Eve and has developed a good relationship with Pope Tawadros II. Symbolic gestures need to be followed by meaningful steps. Despite repeated promises, the Egyptian regime has failed to pass a new law governing the building of houses of worship, which would streamline the process of building churches. Despite proclamations that all of Egypt's citizens are equal, Copts continue to suffer from discrimination in government appointments. Unofficial caps on Coptic representation in key state institutions such as the military and police force continue with several of them such as the intelligence service and the state security not having a single Copt within their ranks. President Sisi needs to change these discriminatory practices and develop a civil service based on merit and not one based on one's faith.

In his speech to scholars of Al Azhar, President Sisi underscored the need for religious reform. The fight against terrorism can no longer be limited to security means, but must be accompanied by a policy tool kit that addresses the root causes of radicalization and terrorism. He has stressed the need to change a religious discourse that has fueled hatred. While President Sisi's call came as a welcome step, the Egyptian regime needs to prove its seriousness by beginning the process of reform. Instead of doing so, the Egyptian state has flipped the call on its head with the Ministry of Religious Endowments forming groups to spread awareness of the threats posed by atheists, Shia and Baha'is.

A good place to start would be Egypt's educational system. Despite numerous attempts at reform, some of which were funded by USAID, Egypt's current educational system is an incubator for extremism and radicalization. Attempting to address the question of intolerance, radicalization, and extremism in the Egyptian educational system must begin by addressing the very structure of that system and not merely changing curricula as previous efforts have attempted. With 24.3% of non-technical high school students in Egypt, Al Azhar managed schools, whose' curriculum teaches intolerance of non-Muslims and helps radicalize students, should be brought under the supervision of the Ministry of Education. Students should not continue being taught that the rules of Dhimmitude are to be upheld, that Christians should pay

Jizya, or that building new churches in the land of Islam is not permissible. Reforming the curriculum should not be based on haphazardly adding a few sections on tolerance and citizenship values to the textbooks, but instead should adopt a cross-disciplinary approach that stresses values of equality, peace, and respect for other views throughout the curriculum. Egyptian schools should no longer produce students who know nothing about the world around them, a void that is only filled by Islamists with falsehoods and conspiracy theories. Students should be taught world history, the history of ideas and world religions and cultures in order for them to understand and respect the richness of diversity, and Egyptian history textbooks should include the important contributions that Christians, Jews and women have made to Egyptian society. On top of all those efforts, attention must be given to educating the teachers themselves given the instrumental role they play in how the curriculum is taught and understood. The Ministry of Education should reverse its policy of transferring extremist teachers to far away governorates in the country's south, making these governorates the perfect recruiting ground for extremists, and ensure that no extremist teacher is allowed in the classroom.

Only by addressing the roots causes of the plight of religious minorities, only by confronting extremism head on by eradicating it from the classrooms, only by upholding the rule of law and treating all of Egypt's citizens as equals without discrimination, and only by preventing the mob attacks on Copts, can Egypt be put on a path towards stability and prosperity. Egypt must undertake these steps and many others, but it will also need the help of its international friends on top of which is the United States.

On the 11th of January 1974, former Secretary of State Henry Kissinger arrived in the Egyptian city of Aswan to begin his shuttle diplomacy between Arab capitals and Jerusalem. While the immediate goal of Dr. Kissinger's diplomatic efforts was ensuring agreement on proposals for disengagement following the 1973 war, the former Secretary soon discovered a willing partner in Egypt's President Anwar El Sadat. In the following years, key American Cold war strategic interests were achieved as President Sadat agreed, in return for the complete return of the Sinai to Egyptian sovereignty not only to seek a lasting peace between his country and Israel, but also to detach Egypt from the Soviet orbit and put it formally in the U.S. camp. In return for U.S. financial, military and developmental assistance, Egypt would become a U.S. ally and successive U.S. administrations hoped that the country would lead the region away from the path of destruction and war introducing a new era of peace and cooperation.

For some thirty years, the formula worked. Despite continued U.S. Egyptian disagreements over a variety of issues ranging from the peace process, U.S. policies in the region, democracy, and human rights, Egypt and the United States developed a close partnership to face a variety of security challenges from Saddam's invasion of Kuwait in 1990, to terrorism. Most importantly, the peace treaty between Egypt and Israel, despite remaining cold, has held.

The Egypt of today is however not the one that Dr. Kissinger has visited in 1974 and with which he built a lasting partnership. Instead of being a regional player leading the region to peace, Egypt has now become a playing field where a variety of international, regional and local forces compete in an all-out war to shape the country's future trajectory. Egypt is no longer a contestant but instead is itself contested. Despite these changes, U.S. policy has not followed suit in addressing the changing conditions. The United States continues to base its policies on an Egypt that no longer exists.

This has to change. As Egypt continues to face severe challenges on various security, economic, and political fronts, the United States needs to adjust its policies towards the country to face those challenges. Instead of hoping for an Egypt that would lead the Middle East to peace, the United States needs to work for an Egypt that does not descend into the regional chaos that has overwhelmed so many Arab countries. U.S. interests in Egypt should no longer be limited to maintaining the peace treaty, securing free passage through the Suez Canal and flights for U.S. military aircrafts in its skies. Instead they should be adjusted to help Egypt face its enduring challenges and overcome them. No one wants a Somalia on the Nile, a Libya on Israel's borders, or a Syria in control of the Suez Canal, the United States least of all.

Thank you again for holding and chairing this hearing and I look forwards to your questions.

Ms. Ros-Lehtinen. Thank you very much.
Dr. Okail.

STATEMENT OF NANCY OKAIL, PH.D., EXECUTIVE DIRECTOR, TAHRIR INSTITUTE FOR MIDDLE EAST POLICY

Ms. Okail. Chairman Ros-Lehtinen, Ranking Member Deutch, and members of the subcommittee, thank you for holding this timely hearing. It is an honor to be here.

Over the past 4 years, Egypt has experienced several waves of instability that have prevented tangible reforms. Unfortunately, in the minds of many, the situation reinforced a false dichotomy between security and economic stability on one hand and democracy and human rights on the other hand.

This also enhanced the view that foreign policy toward Egypt can be viewed in isolation from its domestic affairs. I would like to take this opportunity to clarify the current situation in Egypt and how the U.S. can provide effective support to address it.

We must acknowledge the necessity of the recent U.S. decision to overhaul its aid relationship with Egypt in a way that more appropriately focuses on security and terrorism. However, any assistance provided for these purposes must have rights and good governance as its cornerstone. Otherwise, policies are neither effective nor sustainable.

In 2012, Egypt saw 41 attacks of terror. This year alone, the number has already surpassed 500 attacks. These acts target police, judges, businesses, and increasingly civilians. Some of these acts occur because of domestic motivations, and others are linked to transnational extremism.

In November 2014, a domestic terror group in Sinai, Ansar Bayt al-Maqdis, was welcomed by Islamic State leader Abu Bakr al-Baghdadi as a new province in the so-called Islamic State. In the Western desert region, Egypt's porous border with Libya has caused significant security problems for the country, allowing free flows of arms and in some cases militants in and out of Egypt.

Terror groups continue to successfully expand online, spreading their propaganda and recruiting new members. Many Egyptians have traveled to fight under the Islamic State than are in Iraq, Syria, and Libya, and it is unknown how many have returned home.

Evidently, terror threats are on the rise and require all supports from Egypt's partners. However, the current approach of sweeping arrests, large-scale military campaigns in Sinai, and restrictions on rights and freedom, will not be effective in identifying the actual threats. Physical and cyber threats should not prompt policies of increased surveillance and restrictions of freedom of expression, but, rather, require more open and alternative secular narratives to those of the extremist groups.

Stability cannot occur without accountability and security sector reform. Pervasive evidence of torture, expedited trials, and mass sentencing impede the ability of effective investigation and prosecute legitimate terrorism. Egypt should repeal repressive laws and encourage legal training that will fairly consider the rights of all to due process.

Currently, the political space is highly restricted. Egypt has been functioning for long without an elected legislature, and still no date has yet been set for the parliamentary elections. If the political and public spheres remain closed, people will have no channel for peaceful engagement, and those with grievances will have no recourse, or only violent resource, to communicate their messages.

The current controversial demonstration law severely restricts Egypt's rights to peaceful assembly. Among those who have been arrested under the law are prominent activists and peaceful human rights defenders, including Alaa Abdel Fattah, Ahmed Maher Douma, Yara Sallam, Sanaa Seif. All those committed to transparency and democracy and detained under these laws must be released.

Egyptian civil society remains under threat. As you may know, I and 42 and other received sentences of 1 to 5 years in prison for our work promoting democracy. Since this time proposed drafts for the NGO law have become more restrictive, many Egyptians are now in the same position as I am, living in exile, separated from our families, and unable to go back to our country without fear of serving years in prison. Such intimidation must stop, and the laws must be amended to civil society actors to engage in their important work and receive necessary support from international counterparts.

By recognizing that there can be no security without rights, and no safety without democratic development, the United States has a unique opportunity to support Egypt in restoring its stability in an effective and sustainable way. Specific recommendations for Congress could be found in my written testimony.

Thank you so much, and I look forward to your questions.

[The prepared statement of Ms. Okail follows:]

The Tahrir Institute
for Middle East Policy

Written Testimony of

Dr. Nancy Okail

Executive Director

Tahrir Institute for Middle East Policy

Hearing on

"Egypt Two Years After Morsi: Part I"

before the

Subcommittee on the Middle East and North Africa
of the House Committee on Foreign Affairs

May 20, 2015

Chairman Ros-Lehtinen, Ranking Member Deutch, and members of the Subcommittee, thank you for holding this important hearing to discuss the current human rights and security situation in Egypt since the overthrow of former President Mohamed Morsi in 2013.

Four days ago, on May 16, ousted President Mohamed Morsi and more than one hundred others were sentenced to death for charges of conspiring with foreign militants to free imprisoned Islamists.[1] The same day, three Egyptian judges were shot dead in North Sinai[2] and a policeman was killed on the outskirts of Cairo. The incidents of that day are notable in that they serve as examples of the continuing instability that Egypt faces.

Since the days of hope and inspiration following the January 25, 2011, revolution, Egypt has experienced several waves of instability, which come with many inherent challenges. More than four years after the revolution, these challenges have prevented real, tangible, and significant changes from taking place in Egypt. Unfortunately, in the minds of many, these challenges have also reinforced a false dichotomy between economic stability and security on one hand and democracy and human rights on the other.

History tells us that this assumption is flawed: Egypt, for the longest time, was considered the most stable country in the region and for that reason President Hosni Mubarak was supported for three decades, only to be toppled in only 18 days of popular protests. The 2011 uprisings sent a clear message that there is no enduring stability in the absence of equality, freedom, and democracy. It is clear that Egypt's domestic affairs cannot be ignored or viewed in isolation from regional geopolitical developments and the international policies that seek to address them.

Missing this clear message, international policymakers seem to increasingly accept an approach toward Egypt that prioritizes short-term stability over long-term, sustainable change. Four years after the Arab Spring, a regional landscape dominated by instability, chaos, violence, and the threat of imminent danger that could soon spill over to the rest of the world has created pressure for rapid response—but too often this response comes at the expense of proactive and long-term policy planning. This testimony aims to clarify the current situation in Egypt, the main challenges facing the country, and how the United States can effectively support sustainable progress in Egypt.

The periods following the downfall of Mubarak in 2011 and then of Morsi in 2013 saw moments of instability and insecurity that have provided a fertile environment for the proliferation of security threats in Egypt. The influx of weapons from neighboring Libya, mounting frustrations with leadership and governance, and the ideological capital of transnational jihadism (particularly the rise of the Islamic State since 2011) have all contributed to the rise of terrorism in Egypt.

While Egypt has a clear and pressing need to confront this security threat, an accountable and professional security sector and an independent and impartial judicial system that can be trusted to mete out justice in an even-handed manner must be the foundations of its efforts. The January 25 revolution was triggered by many forms of injustice, primary among them police abuse and brutality. However, throughout the past four years, no systematic approach has been taken to hold those who commit violations accountable or to embark on serious attempt toward police reform. As a result, violations remain numerous.

[1] Mohammed Morsi, Egypt's ex-leader, sentenced to death," BBC (May 16, 2015), *available at* http://www.bbc.com/news/world-middle-east-32763215.

[2] Lizzie Dearden, "Egyptian judges shot dead in Sinai hours after former president Mohamed Morsi sentenced to death," THE INDEPENDENT (May 17, 2015), *available at* http://www.independent.co.uk/news/world/africa/three-egyptian-judges-shot-dead-in-sinai-hours-after-mohamed-morsi-sentenced-to-death-10255067.html.

Effective action by a competent security force cannot be the sole pillar of successful policy to counter security threats in Egypt. When the country faced a wave of terrorism in the 1990s, the state responded with hard-nosed tactics, leaving a wake of repressive policies that ultimately created more grievances than they solved. To avoid the mistakes of the past, Egypt and its international partners have an opportunity to create a lasting stability by enacting policies that consider freedom and democratic development an integral component of security, rather than an obstacle to it.

The Deterioration of Egypt's Security since 2011

In 2012, Egypt saw 41 acts of terror; in 2013 and 2014, the annual count rose to over 330. This year, from January to April 2015 alone, there have already been 442 discrete acts of terror on Egyptian soil. During this time period, we at the Tahrir Institute for Middle East Policy (TIMEP) have documented several trends in the location and nature of attacks. Increasingly, the threat is no longer isolated to the remote and sparsely populated Sinai Peninsula. While nearly all attacks before 2014 occurred in the North Sinai province on Egypt's eastern border with Israel, in the past four months, attacks in this area have accounted for only 31% of all attacks, with Greater Cairo accounting for nearly 20%.

Attacks are also becoming deadlier and civilians are affected by attacks more than ever. The two deadliest months in terms of terror attacks in the past four years were January and April 2015, and each of the first four months of 2015 saw more attacks with civilian casualties than in any other month during the past five years.

Not only is the threat evolving in terms of the number and nature of attacks, but the number and character of the violent actors is changing as well. At the time of cementing its November announcement of allegiance to the Islamic State, Ansar Bayt al-Maqdis refined its propaganda, appearing on social media for the first time and releasing video-recorded executions in the style of its counterparts in Iraq and Syria. The group began to carry out Islamic State-style beheadings. Also, its tactics became more sophisticated, leading to large-scale, coordinated attacks in July, October, and January, which continue today.

In the rest of the country, smaller and sporadic shootings have morphed into targeted assassinations and attacks involving the use of improvised explosive devices, many of which have been carried out by a new coalition of groups that call themselves the Allied Popular Resistance Movement. Groups operating under this banner do not espouse the same jihadist ideology as their analogues; rather, they employ a language of revenge and retribution for those who support a state leadership that they view as illegitimate. They target police, judges, and businesses in order to carry out a violent version of what they call justice.

In the Western Desert region, Egypt's porous border with Libya has caused significant security problems for the country since the downfall of Muammar Qaddafi in 2011. The difficulty in adequately securing a long desert border has allowed for freer flows of arms, and, in some cases, militants into and out of Egypt. In February 2015, a United Nations panel of experts concluded that "Egypt continues to be among the primary destinations for Libyan weapons."[3]

Facing few limitations, Egypt's terror groups and their regional counterparts continue to successfully expand online, spreading their propaganda and recruiting new members. The Islamic State has been especially successful in utilizing the internet for recruitment and the dissemination of its terrorist narrative.

---

[3] United Nations, Security Council, *Final report of the Panel of Experts established pursuant to resolution 1973 (2011)*, S/2015/128 (23 February 2015), *available at* http://www.un.org/ga/search/view_doc.asp?symbol=S/2015/128.

While the exact number is unknown, many Egyptians have traveled to fight under the Islamic State banner in Iraq, Syria, and Libya, and returned home with new knowledge and experience.

As J.M. Berger of the Brookings Institution noted in his recent testimony before the Senate Committee on Homeland Security & Governmental Affairs, the success of terror groups stems in part from their advanced technical capabilities, messaging skills, and in their ability to take advantage of the inter-connectivity of social media.[4] By using social media to spread propaganda and connect to potential recruits, terror groups have been able to provide social context and a validation of beliefs for would-be terrorists, allowing them to easily become part of a group and making them more likely to mobilize in the name of IS. Because of its size, IS can afford to have several thousand members tweeting several times a day and can offer two or three recruiters for each potential recruit. Although it may be used nefariously, the potential for connectivity has also been used for constructive political means; many positive policy changes have been triggered by public pressure channeled through social media campaigns, and in this way, social media represents an effective medium for accountability.

Considering these security trends and challenges facing Egypt, we at TIMEP acknowledge the necessity of the Obama administration's recent decision to overhaul its aid relationship with Egypt in a way that more appropriately focuses on security and terrorism. By ending Egypt's cash flow financing in fiscal year 2018 and directing U.S.-funded military aid for Egypt toward counterterrorism and border security equipment and training, the United States will be better positioned to assist Egypt in a way that reflects both countries' shared security interests. However, the United States must ensure that any assistance provided for security or counterterrorism purposes to Egypt will not be used irresponsibly or allow for crackdown on peaceful opposition.

At the same time, efforts to tackle Egypt's immediate security threats must be accompanied by a long-term strategy to meaningfully address Egypt's endemic social, economic, and political problems. While Egypt has not yet succumbed to widespread violence and insecurity in the way that other countries in the region have, it is not immune to that fate. The United States must work with leadership in Egypt to reform its human rights practices, continue to support education initiatives, and implement the democratic reforms for which so many Egyptians have risked—and lost—their lives.

Structural Reforms Needed to Achieve Security in Egypt

Internally, Egypt needs to urgently address the following longstanding, structural challenges that have undermined civil and political rights:

- **Enhance the rule of law and open up political space**

At the crux of any reform that will adequately address the aforementioned concerns lies a need for trust in the rule of law, a fully-functioning and effective elected legislature, and confidence in the judiciary. In the absence of a parliamentary body to carry out the legislative functions of the state, President Abdel-Fattah El Sisi has enjoyed both executive and legislative authority since his inauguration on June 8, 2014. While many of his legislative decrees have fallen well within constitutional requirements to ensure the function and prosperity of the nation, a number of controversial laws that implicate citizens' freedoms and rights have been passed, including the University Law and the foreign funding amendments to the penal code.

---

[4] U.S. Senate, Committee on Homeland Security & Governmental Affairs. *Jihad 2.0: Social Media in the Next Evolution of Terrorist Recruitment*, Hearing, May 7, 2015, at 35:00, *available at* http://www.hsgac.senate.gov/hearings/jihad-20-social-media-in-the-next-evolution-of-terrorist-recruitment.

Such legislation should be the product of extensive debate and research through an elected parliamentary body and ultimately should be a reflection of the will of the people.

- **Promote accountability and professionalism in the security sector**

One of the sparks of the uprising in 2011 was the brutal beating and death of Khaled Said at the hands of police. Graphic photos of Said's bloodied and disfigured face prompted many to take to the streets, fed up with the impunity of police abuse. Today, there seems to have been little progress in police reform, and allegations of brutal beatings, sexual abuse, and electric shock are particularly common among prisoners in Egypt's detention facilities. Despite the many protections against such abuse afforded by Egypt's constitution, these laws are weakly enforced, leaving many torture victims deprived of justice.

Accountability for abuse is rare, though it does occur. In May 2015, Egypt's Court of Cassation upheld a sentence against 14 policemen for torturing to death two prisoners in 2006.[5] Twenty-six year old Karim Hamdy, a lawyer, was tortured to death at the same police station in February 2015.[6] Two police officers are currently standing trial for Hamdy's death, yet impunity seems to be the norm when it comes to police abuse and violence, and those who advocate for police reform face an uphill battle. A recent attempt by two Egyptian judges to propose a law that would criminalize the use of torture in police stations and detention facilities resulted in their being referred to investigation.[7]

Rather than a few sporadic and largely symbolic instances of accountability, deep and comprehensive security sector reform is critical. Human rights and professionalism training must be integral to all levels of police and military training, not only for the officer corps. Gaining the respect of citizens, rather than their animosity, will better allow security forces to address true threats to public safety, and not be the source of them.

- **Create and protect spaces of public engagement where dissent may be peaceably expressed**

In November 2013, then-Interim President Adly Mansour signed into effect a controversial law that effectively banned street protests, severely restricting Egyptians' right to peaceful assembly and freedom of expression. Since its adoption, the law has been used to target several prominent activists and political opposition members. Among those who have been arrested under the law are activists and peaceful human rights defenders who participated in the revolution and engaged in critical opposition to injustices during all periods of rule since and before the time of Mubarak. These include Alaa Abdel Fattah, Ahmed Maher, Ahmed Douma, Yara Sallam, Sanaa Seif Mohamed, and several others.

Prominent activist and blogger Alaa Abdel Fattah was sentenced in February 2015 for violating the protest law, and is presently serving a five-year prison term and is to pay a fine of 100,000 Egyptian pounds (over $13,000 USD). Women human rights defenders have equally been targeted by this law. Lawyer and activist Yara Sallam and activist Sanaa Seif, who have been detained since June 21, 2014, were sentenced in October 2014 along with nearly two dozen other activists and are presently serving a

---

[5] "Egypt court upholds sentences against 14 policemen for torture, AHRAM (May 3, 2015), *available at* http://english.ahram.org.eg/NewsContent/1/64/129272/Egypt/Politics-/Egypt-court-upholds-sentences-against-policemen-f.aspx.

[6] "Autopsy shows lawyer was tortured to death at Matareya police station," MADA MASR (Feb. 27, 2015), *available at* http://www.madamasr.com/news/autopsy-shows-lawyer-was-tortured-death-matareya-police-station.

[7] "Egypt investigates judges for drafting anti-torture bill," AL ARABY, April 20, 2015, *available at* http://www.alaraby.co.uk/english/news/2015/4/21/egypt-investigates-judges-for-drafting-anti-torture-bill.

two-year prison sentence for violating the law. Additionally, award-winning human rights lawyer Mahinour El-Masry was sentenced and served a six-month jail term for violating the law.

By jailing peaceful protestors and restricting the rights of all to public space, Egypt has cut the state's ability to hear grievances at the knees. Public demonstration should signal an urgent need for reform measures, and by curtailing it, advocates have no recourse—or only violent recourse—to express their message. For these reasons, Egypt must urgently repeal its protest law and immediately release those unjustly detained and sentenced pursuant to it.

- **Foster transparency through diverse and independent media**

After the 2011 uprising, many new voices were heard across Egypt's television and radio waves, sparking new conversations about politics and society. This trend has been halted, and may even be reverting back to the restrictive environment that we saw prior to 2011. Today, many journalists face intimidation or arrests—such as photojournalist Mahmoud Abou Zeid (a.k.a. "Shawkan"), who has been detained for over 600 days without trial—or face other forms of punishment for attempting to bring valued information to the Egyptian public. Those who are not directly targeted by the government may nevertheless censor themselves for fear of punitive consequences.

While the Egyptian state has a commitment to ensuring the professionalism of media that is not used to disseminate hate speech, this must not supersede its commitment to ensuring freedom of expression and information. At a bare minimum, those imprisoned for their commitment to government transparency must be released, and specific legislation must outline definitions for hate speech.

- **Engage with civil society counterparts as essential partners in governance**

Egyptian civil society is currently facing serious challenges. The changing political leadership and climate in Egypt over the past three years tightened the grip on freedom of association throughout the country since the crackdown on foreign nongovernmental organizations (NGOs) working in Egypt put 43 individuals on trial in 2012. Twenty-seven of the defendants, including myself, were sentenced *in absentia* and received prison sentences of five years, while five others received two-year prison sentences and eleven others received one-year suspended sentences. Many of the Egyptian defendants in this case—like me—are now living in exile, separated from our families and unable to return to our country due to the likelihood that we will be forced to spend years behind bars in service to these unjust sentences.

In September 2014, Egypt's penal code was amended to increase the penalties for those who seek or receive foreign funding for the broad purpose of undermining national interests. The failure to define national interests or acts which may undermine these means the law risks an overly broad and indiscriminate application. The new penalties would impose up to a life sentence (25 years, under Egyptian law) and fines of no less than 500,000 Egyptian pounds (about $66,000 USD). The overly obscure language in the law makes it possible for it to be applied in a repressive manner, creating an environment of fear among those in civil society.

The Egyptian government should realize that civil society is not the enemy, and should consult with, rather than punish, Egyptian NGOs. Restrictions that allow for invasive monitoring of NGO activities should be lifted, and the penal code must be amended to allow civil society actors the freedom to engage in their important work without fear of spending their life behind bars or in exile.

- **Recognize and address the struggles of marginalized groups, including women, minorities, and the poor**

Insecurity, instability, and terrorism are always felt most acutely by already vulnerable populations, such as women, religious and ethnic minorities, and the poor. A vision for security that includes all Egyptians undoubtedly requires recognizing the ongoing struggle of Egypt's marginalized groups.

For women, this means—at minimum—making it safe for them to go out in public. According to a 2013 study by UN Women, an estimated 99.3% of Egyptian women have experienced sexual harassment.[8] Often this harassment leads to brutal outcomes, as Egypt saw following the horrific June 2014 video of a woman being gang-raped in Tahrir Square. .

Like women, religious minorities must confront ongoing challenges as they attempt to weave themselves into Egypt's social and political fabric. For many Egyptians, the right to mere religious identity presents a daily—and for some, existential—struggle. Religious freedom in Egypt remains elusive, particularly as leadership has declared its intent to establish Egypt as a protector of "moderate Islam."[9] While some have praised a commitment to moderation in the face of extremism, the state's increasing role as arbiter of moral authority has had devastating implications for minority identity communities. Additionally, this commitment to moderate Islam has come hand in hand with unfulfilled promises for meaningful religious reform.

If Egyptian state leadership and state religious institutions mean to address tendencies toward extremism in Egypt's Muslim communities, the first step must be taken with examination of the theological tendencies of state institutions themselves. Al-Azhar, Egypt's foremost religious authority, continues to harbor religious perspectives that are imperceptible from the extremists the country aims to combat. Rather than prescribing moral authenticity, Egypt's religious and state leaders should promote meaningful dialogue that explores and raises awareness about non-normative religious and identity values.

Access to adequate housing, water, sanitation, and education and health facilities plague the 26% of Egypt's population living in poverty. While their grievances have provided fodder for the recruitment of terrorists, Egypt's poor should not be viewed as suspicious criminals but for their potential contributions to Egyptian society, as Egypt's next doctors, lawyers, artists, leaders, and, yes, judges, waiting for their rightful opportunities.

The U.S. Can Play a Critical Role in Promoting a Balance between Security and Freedom in Egypt

The United Sates must recognize the integral importance of rights and freedoms for bilateral strategic interests, and this must form the foundation of the U.S. relationship with Egypt. Not only will this help to secure U.S. economic and security interests in the region, but if carried out with diligence, deliberation, and earnest commitment, the United States may additionally repair a negative image in the country.

---

[8] "Study on Ways and Methods to Eliminate Sexual Harassment in Egypt," UN WOMEN (2014), *available at* http://harassmap.org/en/wp-content/uploads/2014/02/287_Summaryreport_eng_low-1.pdf.
[9] "El-Sissi: Egypt a 'beacon of moderate Islam'," PBS NEWS HOUR (Sept. 24, 2014), *available at* https://www.youtube.com/watch?v=3GZjfzV_dx4.

Several objectives should provide the foundation for U.S.-Egypt bilateral relations:

1. *Encourage swift parliamentary elections in adherence with Egypt's constitutional and international legal obligations.*

In the absence of an elected legislature, any discussion of inclusive reform policies in Egypt is meaningless, as reform will remain the legal responsibility of the president alone. While President Sisi has a responsibility to continue to enact legislation that pertains to the functioning of the nation, he has publicly declared his intent to hold elections promptly. However, elections have been postponed several times, and at the time of testimony, no date had yet been set for them.

The United States must highlight the necessity of free and fair elections for good governance. While these are not the only requirements for democracy, elections are important for opening political space for all, not just for one oppressed group. This is particularly important as many of the nascent political actors that emerged after the 2011 revolution face an existential threat now that their resources have been drained after years of delayed democracy.

2. *Strengthen rule of law through transitional justice programs and judicial reform.*

Weaknesses in the judicial process and pervasive impunity undermine the rule of law, both for those who believe their status places them above the law or those who believe the law will never be on their side. The United States must pressure Egypt to repeal repressive laws and should encourage legal training for judges that emphasizes the right of all to due process. This is of utmost importance in combating terrorism, as the pervasive evidence of torture, expedited trials under a military judicial system, and mass sentencing impede the judiciary's ability to effectively investigate and prosecute legitimate terrorism. The United States should recognize these weaknesses and advocate for their reform.

3. *Press for security sector reform with requisite human rights and professionalism training and accountability measures.*

A fundamental component of transitional justice in Egypt must be the reform of the security sector and accountability for security sector abuses of justice. The few but public trials in which police have been held responsible for their offenses is a step in the right direction for accountability, but ultimately those offenses must not only be punished, but prevented. Requisite trainings on internationally-accepted standards on use of force, the letter of the law surrounding human rights, and best practices to enforce law among vulnerable populations should be implemented at every level of police and military training. The United States, which already partners with Egypt on training programs, should augment these and conduct regular review to ensure programs' efficacy.

4. *Target security measures to known cyber- and physical threats, rather than engaging in indiscriminate crackdowns.*

Egypt's current war on terror been characterized by sweeping arrests, large-scale military campaigns in the Sinai Peninsula, and restrictions on freedoms of expression, associations, and assembly. Not only is this approach ineffective in identifying actual threats, it risks fostering acrimony toward the state, potentially creating future terrorists. Specific definitions of terrorism are necessary to ensure targeting of credible threats, and law enforcement should focus on threats based on thorough investigation.

Additionally, recognizing the power of technology at the hands of extremists, policymakers must devote efforts to combating extremism online. These efforts require a counter-narrative to extremism, one which should not necessarily be religiously-based but that speaks to and address the demands and objectives of youth, who represent such a critical demographic in the region. Contrary to current calls, the current cyber threat should not prompt policies of increased surveillance and restriction on freedom of expression, but rather expand this space for more open and alternative narratives to those of the extremist groups.

Recommendations to the U.S. Government

To support the objectives and further the policy approach outlined here, the U.S. government can urge a more careful and strategic rebalancing of Egypt's security challenges and human rights obligation in a number of ways:

Consider a Recalibration of U.S. Aid Levels

- Congress should require the State Department, in consultation with the Defense Department and the U.S. Agency for International Development (USAID), to conduct a multi-year strategic review of military and economic aid to Egypt to assess whether current funding levels—as well as the administration's recently proposed changes to U.S. aid to Egypt—effectively advance human rights and democracy reform in Egypt, support Egypt's economic growth, and meet the United States and Egypt's mutual national security interests.

Demand Greater Respect for Fundamental Rights

- The U.S. government must continue to urge Egyptian officials to relax or abolish current restrictions placed on civil society organizations and workers by, among other things:

  - requesting assurances that the aforementioned foreign funding restrictions and penalties will not be applied to civil society organizations or workers—particularly those whom USAID and the State Department work with to implement U.S. aid programs—for engaging in legitimate civil society activities protected under international law;
  - insisting that efforts to implement the 2002 NGO law be suspended and that Egypt's parliament, once elected, immediately set out to draft a new associations law that complies with international human rights law;
  - urging, in every meeting with Egyptian officials and at every level, that all civil society workers currently detained under the protest law or for otherwise exercising their fundamental human rights be immediately and unequivocally released and charges against them dropped, and that the right to freedom of association be protected in accordance with international law;
  - urging as well that journalists detained for doing their jobs are immediately and unconditionally released and charges against them are dropped, and that members of the press be permitted to work without interference;
  - demanding that all charges be dropped and sentences commuted for the 43 NGO workers; and
  - ensuring that *all* religious minorities in Egypt are accorded equal rights, and that the "blasphemy" law in Egypt's penal code be repealed.

<u>Ensure that U.S. Military Assistance is Used Responsibly</u>

- The White House has recently announced several significant and much-needed changes to its military aid relationship with Egypt. Going forward, the United States must ensure that any future military aid provided to Egypt is used appropriately and for legitimate defense, security, and/or counterterrorism purposes, and that it is not used indiscriminately against civilian populations.

By recognizing that there can be no security without rights, and no safety without democratic development, the United States has a unique opportunity not to establish its own values in the region, but to offer the crucial support for the millions of Egyptians who proved in 2011 that they too hold these values dear.

Ms. ROS-LEHTINEN. Thank you so much. Thank you to all of our panelists for their great testimony.

Egypt is strategically important for the stability of the region, for helping to contain Iran's push for regional dominance, and for helping counter the terror threats that are coming from Sinai and Libya.

However, many Egyptians have viewed the United States negatively since they see the Obama administration as having supported Morsi and the Muslim Brotherhood. During the 1½ years when the administration remained on the fence about what to do with its Egypt policy, Cairo received billions from its Gulf allies and signed massive arms deals with Russia and with France.

So, Dr. Trager, what does this mean for our relationship and our leverage with Cairo? What does it mean for our long-term national security interests if Egypt and others move away from the United States toward Russia and toward other countries? And as we have heard, terror attacks have increased rapidly in Egypt in the past 2 years. To what do you attribute this rise? And how can Cairo improve its counterterrorism operations? And who are the groups? What are their goals?

Mr. TRAGER. So our leverage with Cairo, as it pertains to shaping their domestic politics I think is very, very limited due to the domestic struggle within that country, the ''kill or be killed'' dynamic that has really defined the politics of the post-Morsi era.

And when we tried to shape that by withholding military aid or much of the military aid, as you said, you know, Egypt gravitated toward Russia, signed a preliminary arms deal with Russia, $3.5 billion. It also signed, I believe, a $5.4 billion deal with France. And that suggests that, you know, this idea within Washington that Egypt won't have other options, needs us, and will, therefore, respond to U.S. pressure as it pertains to its domestic political situation, just isn't true.

And I think we should learn from the experience of the previous 2 years in which we tried to use the military aid as a stick, and, you know, Egypt simply went a different direction. And for sure if Egypt gravitates more toward Russia, or gravitates toward other— you know, other powers for its military aid, that will make it even more difficult for the United States to shape what it has to shape, which is Egypt's foreign relations and Egypt's external policies.

Now, the rise in terrorism within Egypt, especially since Morsi's ouster, I think is attributable to many different things. First of all, Morsi took a pretty light hand in the Sinai, and the theory of the Muslim Brotherhood was that by winning power through elections and working to implement the sharia, which is the Brotherhood's long-term goal, they would convince Sinai jihadis to lay down their arms and adopt the Muslim Brotherhood's path to power.

And in former Secretary of State Hillary Clinton's memoirs, she recounts a conversation with President Morsi in which he said that basically there would be no Sinai attacks under an Islamist president, which clearly was not true. So part of it is the light hand that Morsi took in the Sinai, and the fact that after Morsi was ousted the jihadis feared the return of the security state to Sinai, and then there was an uptick in violence that spread west across the Suez Canal, with major attacks in some of the major Egyptian cities, particularly a massive attack in Mansura, I believe in December 2013.

The other aspect of the recent attacks seems to be the role of Muslim Brotherhood youths in slowly gravitating toward a more aggressive posture vis-a-vis the regime. These tend to not be the mass-scale attacks. They tend to be IED attacks, attacks on infrastructure, attacks on police stations.

It does not seem to me that the Brotherhood has made that decision to attack civilians, and there is actually a very interesting paper written by the former vice chair of the Muslim Brotherhood's political party to this effect that I would be happy to share with the committee.

Now, I need to hedge a little bit and say that we don't have ironclad proof that this is the Muslim Brotherhood, or these are Muslim Brothers. The evidence is circumstantial, but is reflected in Facebook postings and in various interviews that I have had since Morsi's ouster. And the unfortunate thing is, if it is the case, as I frankly believe it is, that the Muslim Brotherhood is involved in these sort of low profile attacks, that is going to be very hard for the current regime to reverse in sort of a negotiated way, because the conflict between the current government and the Brotherhood is existential. There is really no room for compromise between the two. So, you know, my expectation is that Egypt is going to have a very difficult path moving forward.

And just one final point that the ultimate effect of these attacks, and the ultimate effect of the declining security situation, seems to reinforce support for Sisi. And this repressiveness that we have been discussing today, you know, has some significant societal support as a result of both the local context and the regional context. Thank.

Ms. ROS-LEHTINEN. Thank you.

And, Dr. Okail, as we know, Egypt has constitutional, international obligations to hold parliamentary elections, which you were talking about, and you pointed out they have been postponed, they have been delayed for too long now. And last month Sisi declared that these elections would not happen before Ramadan, which begins next month, so another delay.

You point out that these elections could open the political space for all, but they are—and there are now some beginning steps of political actors who emerged after the 2011 revolution, but they are running out of resources. What indications do we have now that there are political groups and players who can organize, who have the capability to not only win an election and form parties but to govern effectively and in a manner that would be free and fair and representative of all the needs of the Egyptian people?

Ms. OKAIL. Thank you, Madam Chairman. I do believe that there are actually new players in the political field in Egypt. And there are several political parties that started to be, I mean, organized and shaped after the revolution. However, as you rightly point out, they are running out of resources, and they are being restricted.

The elections would allow this opportunity of the people to be encouraged to actually engage in a real—I mean, channels into political participation. However, we must look at the overall environment. In order for these political parties to campaign freely, to actually voice their own agendas and their programs and their aspirations for Egypt, they have to have an ability to voice their demands through peaceful channels, like, for example, having a free media, which is currently suffering a lot of restrictions.

At the same time, we should have also independent organizations that would monitor and oversee these processes, which is basically civil society organizations who are currently under restriction because of the current NGO law. And the draft that has been proposed for these organizations to function under a new law has been equally restrictive.

In addition, there was also a new amendment in the penal code that would penalize and criminalize anyone who would receive funding from foreign sources that would—using language that is very loose and just threatens national security, without saying or identifying what would be actually determined and identified as a threat to national security.

All of this put all the players, whether the political actors, the political parties as organized entities, and also analysts and media and civil society actors, under threat and in limbo, and acting under intimidation, which would not be conducive for real environment for an effective elections.

Thank you.

Ms. ROS-LEHTINEN. Thank you very much.

Mr. Deutch is recognized for his questions.

Mr. DEUTCH. Thank you, Madam Chairman.

I would throw this out to the panel. Mr. Tadros, you made yourself clear that you don't believe that at this point, if I understood you correctly, that Egypt can be a leader in the Arab world. To the contrary, I think is how you explained it.

I would just like the panel to look out over the next year or 2 and tell us where you think things are going. We speak in—you know, we focus on different silos and security issues, on human rights issues and civil society. But they are all—they all ultimately impact not just the people of Egypt, but they impact the ability of Egypt to be a leader in the Arab world. They impact the relationship between Egypt and the United States.

So what will things look like a year or 2 out? And to what extent does there necessarily need to be progress on all of these areas for Egypt to be a leader in the Arab world, and do we need to see the same advances for the relationship between Egypt and the United States to be strengthened?

Mr. TADROS. I am indeed making the case that the Egypt with which Dr. Kissinger forged a lasting relationship with the United States is no longer there. The Egypt that was ruled by President Anwar Sadat in 1974 when he first met with Dr. Kissinger was an Egypt that was the cultural leader of the Arab world, that its influence ranged from Morocco to Iraq. It could influence the decisions of the regimes there and lead the region into something.

That is no longer the case. Egypt has deteriorated throughout the past 30 years dramatically on all fronts, whether—it is not only the political stagnation of the Mubarak regime, but it also declined in the role that it played in the regional affairs, surpassed by countries like Qatar and Saudi Arabia, now by the UAE. Others have come up and played that role in the region, leading it with various directions.

The current situation in Egypt is an Egypt that is divided. It is divided along political lines. There is a fight for the soul of Egypt, and a country that is being torn apart between two groups is hardly one capable of projecting power or influence abroad.

The Egyptian—oh, Egypt is today dependent on Gulf countries for economic support for feeding the Egyptian people themselves. It needs those countries' support. It follows Gulf policies in the situation in Yemen and others. It needs the UAE in order to be involved in this situation in Libya. It has no ties to Hamas or the one representative or one group within Palestine.

Historically, the Egyptian regime has been able to play the role of peacemaker between Israel and between Hamas and other terrorist organizations in Gaza. Nowadays, that is no longer possible. Egypt is no longer able to be the peacemaker between them. So on all fronts, I think the ability of Egypt to project power abroad has decreased.

Mr. DEUTCH. But, Dr. Trager, there is an argument to be made, isn't there, that in facing the regional security threats, Egypt is playing a more assertive role. How can—when Mr. Tadros talks about the fight for the soul of Egypt, how does the ''kill or be killed'' struggle that you describe influence all of the other decision-making? And can Egypt move—does that ''kill or be killed'' struggle continue until there is a clear victor? Or have we already reached that point and we are seeing that in the actions that Egypt has been taking on regional security?

Mr. TRAGER. Well, look, I mean, I think the ''kill or be killed'' struggle really refers to the domestic political situation. Sitting here 6,000 miles away, my sense, and perhaps your sense as well, is that it has been settled. I mean, you know, President Sisi has for the most part, and the government, vanquished the Muslim Brotherhood.

But the fact that you have the rise in IED attacks, the fact that you have the Muslim Brotherhood's official language toward the regime becoming much more violent, talking about martyrdom and jihad, I think means that that struggle is going to continue. And it is going to be very hard to move or encourage the domestic politics to move in a more positive direction.

Now, how that hinges on the regional level, it means that Egypt is going to be more aggressive, and President Sisi has spoken about this, against radical Islamic groups, particularly jihadis. The Egyptian role in Yemen, though, is slightly different. There Egypt is trying to protect Bab-el-Mandeb, which is the strait that leads to the Red Sea that leads to the Suez Canal. The Suez Canal is a major source of revenue for Egypt.

So, you know, for now the Egyptian operation there is limited, and I suspect that Egypt will actually play a slightly more conservative role, certainly a more active role in the region than previous governments. But because of the—you know, but a more conservative role than we would expect. It is focusing primarily on strait access in Bab-el-Mandeb, and it is focusing on countering jihadis from Libya.

I don't personally expect Egypt to send ground troops into Yemen. They may send, you know, to Saudi Arabia to protect the border, but I—you know, maybe I will be proven wrong here, but I don't think that we are going to see a significant Egyptian military role beyond those kind of more narrow interests.

Mr. DEUTCH. Dr. Okail, I am out of time, but I hope as we go forward you will have a chance to talk about the extent to which Egypt will or will not be able to exert a greater role in the region while some of the domestic issues continue to be hashed out. But for now, I will yield back.

Ms. ROS-LEHTINEN. Mr. Rohrabacher is recognized.

Mr. ROHRABACHER. Thank you very much, Madam Chairman. And, again, thank you for holding this hearing today and drawing our attention to a country and a struggle that is vital not only to that country but in the long run to the rest of that region and to the world and to the people of the United States.

I believe it is just that historic an event that we are looking at that if we do not do what is right could lead to a historic catastrophe in the sense of the instability and the bloodshed that it could create on a global scale. Because if Egypt—as I mentioned earlier, if Egypt falls to radical Islam, the other countries in the Gulf, with their enormous wealth and power, would be transferred to a radical Islamic goal, which would be a catastrophe for our country and for the Western civilization and for the people of that region.

So I say Egypt is now playing a positive role, even though it is less of a role, in that region because it is taking care of their business at home. Are we being as supportive as we should be to President al-Sisi in his efforts to, number one, create a stable Egypt, and, number two, make sure that Egypt has the weapons and the equipment necessary to play a positive role in that region?

Now, could I have a short answer from each of the witnesses on that?

Mr. TRAGER. Well, thank you very much. I mean, I think that we could be doing more in terms of, you know, expressing our partnership with Egypt on certain strategic issues. I think in terms of validating the domestic political trajectory that should be a bridge too far for us. You know, we have reasonable concerns about the political trajectory there, the repression. There are very reasonable concerns about whether that will, you know, actually help the situation.

I do think we have a very limited ability to shape that, so I would urge Congress to urge the administration to move forward with the strategic dialogue with Egypt to get the aid and military-to-military relationship back on track.

Mr. ROHRABACHER. Let me note from that answer, President al-Sisi has not received the weapons that he was expected. He just recently obtained some helicopters from the United States and find out that they did not have the defensive measures on the helicopters that were necessary for them to be used to thwart a radical Islamic insurgency or some kind of an attack out in the Libyan end of their country.

That is disgraceful on our part, Madam Chairman, to give weapons systems that they can't even use. It is a slap in his face. As well as the spare parts for the tanks that his country needs, if there is a problem in—especially out in the Libyan end of his country, this is outrageous.

And the fact that the Russians have come in and given al-Sisi some support, here is where I disagree with my colleagues, I think that is a good thing that the Russians are helping President al-Sisi, and I think that we should take that into consideration on how we judge Russia instead of considering it always the enemy of the United States.

Sir, would you like to answer the first question about, are we playing the supportive role we should be?

Mr. TADROS. Certainly. As the Congressman has mentioned, Egypt is important, not because it will play a regional role, but because the fate of Egypt should be a concern to the United States, a country of 19 million people, a country that borders Israel, that is in control of the Suez Canal. For all those reasons, the U.S. needs to be actively involved in investing in Egypt's future, making sure that Egypt does not fall to the same regional upheaval that has taken so many countries there.

But this is not only limited to military investment in Egypt's future, bolstering its military capabilities against the security threat, but also investing in Egypt's development, in Egypt's other challenges, in Egypt's rule of law, in building Egyptian institutions that are representatives of their citizens, that are welcomed by their citizens, that is a venue for their citizens to bring about their concerns to their leadership in order for that country not to collapse the same way as other countries have.

Unfortunately, the United States has not been doing that. For so long, the administration has been tied to this question of, was it a coup or was it not a coup? What do we do with the military aid? And has forgotten about the other aspects of the relationship, that it is not only about the military aid but about other things as well.

Mr. ROHRABACHER. Very good answer. Could we have a quick answer, Madam Chairman, with indulgence, could our last witness—have her comment on that?

Ms. OKAIL. Thank you. I think one issue to clarify right here is that so far the conversation is limited to government-to-government relationship. However, as President Obama mentioned in his speech after the Egyptian uprising and said, it is time to stand on the right side of history and side with the people. This has not translated into actual policies, because right now it is confined between military-to-military relationship, without actual engagement with the Egyptian people.

And this is—Madam Chairman, answers your question about the reputation of the United States within the—and the sentiments of the Egyptian people because they did not actually feel that there is real engagement. And this can only happen and translate into actual policies when there are support and finances and resources that are channeled toward the civil society organizations that represent the people.

The other point, just to say very briefly, that with the changing leadership in Egypt in terms of the personality of the president, there are beyond that inherent structural challenges for the Egyptian state itself. The institutions that actually suffered under Mubarak have not actually undergone real structural reforms, and I am speaking here about the police, the security sector, and the judiciary itself. And it has, as we have seen, the same even particular people who are drafting the laws under Mubarak are the same people who were drafting the laws under Morsi and until today, and this needs to change to actually lead to real structural change and development.

Thank you.

Mr. ROHRABACHER. Thank you.

Thank you, Madam Chairman.

Ms. ROS-LEHTINEN. Thank you, Mr. Rohrabacher.

Mr. Connolly.

Mr. CONNOLLY. Thank you, Madam Chairman.

Dr. Trager, I mentioned sort of three areas it seems to me we need to be concerned about with respect to Egypt. But backing up just a little bit, you indicated, and, as you may know, our State Department has said that the Muslim Brotherhood, led by Morsi, won a free and fair election.

Now, if the United States is going to have credibility in the region in encouraging others to move toward a democratic form of government, our tacit support for military overthrow of a duly elected government, albeit one we felt was on the wrong track, and guilty of some serious missteps with respect to writing a constitution protecting minority rights, and the like, nonetheless, doesn't that sort of damage our credibility in the region as we try to encourage others to move in a democratic path?

Mr. TRAGER. Thank you for your question. I would argue that the credibility of democracy in the region, unfortunately, doesn't rest on our statements and our policies. It, frankly, rests on the performance of those who are elected. And Morsi's failure in power, the fact that he used an election to grab more power through an edict, that he rammed through a very controversial Islamist constitution, that he failed economically, that the Muslim Brotherhood mobilized its cadres to attack protesters, that he tried to crack down on media, and if the country was really sliding into an abyss—and, frankly, still has many, many challenges—I would argue that all of those things significantly undermined, you know, the credibility of democracy within Egypt. And it is very hard for us to rescue that from there.

And I say that, by the way, very sadly, but——

Mr. CONNOLLY. Would you cite the current military government, albeit elected, as the alternative? I mean, is that a paragon of democratic virtue in the region?

Mr. TRAGER. I am certainly not arguing that it is.

Mr. CONNOLLY. Do you believe that the current government is committed to the rule of law?

Mr. TRAGER. I think that there are major challenges regarding the rule of law. I think the current government is faced with significant institutional challenges, and the power struggle that has, frankly, defined Egypt's post-Mubarak trajectory since 2011 is still playing out, and we see that today in tensions between the presidency and the Interior Ministry and the power of the judiciary. I mean, this is still a regime that is defining itself.

I agree with you very much that the trajectory is not democratic. All that I am arguing is our capacity to shape that is almost non-existent.

Mr. CONNOLLY. Yes. One of the things I think we should have learned from the overthrow of the Shah of Iran is that when you don't allow the creation of political space, then you can't be surprised at the rise of an element we don't like, because—and in the case of Egypt, years of repression of the political space it seems to me made the Muslim Brotherhood the only alternative to the regime, and nothing in between particularly. And that is why they won the election.

And it seems to me that the current military government, in going all out in this existential battle for survival you referred to, may unwittingly exacerbate the situation we are concerned about by not allowing political space. Even NGOs not allowed to function and being pilloried and persecuted for democratic expression of ideals.

Your comment on that.

Mr. TRAGER. Well, that is clearly, you know, very possible. And it is true that, look, we should be deeply concerned about Egypt's domestic trajectory, and we should be communicating that very, very clearly. I think that the Secretary of State made a huge mistake when he said that Egypt is on a transition toward democracy. That is just not accurate.

But at the same time, I think we have to be conservative in what we can expect from Egypt under the current circumstances of a great deal of violence domestically, a deteriorating regional situation. And, moreover, we should acknowledge the fact of the past 4½ years, which is that political change comes from many different, you know, sources, but the ultimate decider, for lack of a better word, of that change is the military, and that has been for, you know, over 40 years our partner in Egypt.

Mr. CONNOLLY. If the chair would allow just Mr. Tadros or Dr. Okail to also respond to that.

Mr. TADROS. I would be happy to. We certainly cannot influence—the United States cannot influence Egypt's relationship or the Egyptian regime's relationship with the Muslim Brotherhood. It can, however, influence other aspects that are not life and death issues through the Egyptian regime.

So the fate of former President Morsi is one issue where we cannot comment on or affect, because simply President Sisi realizes that if the Brotherhood ever took power again, it is his life that will be there. He will be the one hanged.

There are many other issues on the domestic front where the United States, partnering with Egypt, can influence these things to a better direction, whether it is talking building the rule of law, building state institutions, representative governments. We might not be able to force them to hold free and fair elections, but we can certainly train the judges better, we can help the police force deal with protests much better without killing protesters. There are many areas that can be worked on.

Mr. CONNOLLY. And, Dr. Okail, if you could briefly comment. Thank you, Madam Chairman.

Ms. OKAIL. Yes, please. I just want to underscore that, again, most of the conversations focus on the physical interactions, I mean, security physically on the ground and limiting the ability of people to physically assemble and demonstrate, forgoing that during this year and age, and this time, that the internet plays a very important role, and this cannot be restricted as the ability of the security forces could do in the streets in shooting people dead.

And we have seen also cases where, if the security is the prime objective that we want to achieve, we have seen cases, for example, that one of the defendants who was just sentenced to death, for example, he was an average, normal young Egyptian citizen, got radicalized by connection with some of those terror groups, traveled to Syria, got trained there, and came back and participated in an organization who are planning to conduct some terror attacks, in just less than 6 months.

This is how quick and this is how volatile the situation can be. And this is just one example to give you, that if we just follow the security approach it will not really lead to stability or security. And that opening the space for more alternative narratives to those of the extremist groups, that would actually be the only answer for that to be defeated, both on the cyber battlefield and on the ground.

Thank you.

Ms. ROS-LEHTINEN. Thank you so much.

Mr. Webber is recognized.

Mr. WEBBER. The gentleman from Virginia always has such good questions. I could sit and listen to him all day, and, like a lot of you, I thought I was going to have to.

Just a joke, Gerry. Just a joke.

You all didn't respond to the gentleman from California's comments about him thinking that Russia being involved in helping Egypt was a good thing. Dr. Trager, how do you—what say you?

Mr. TRAGER. I mean, I respectfully disagree that Russia strengthening its relationship with Egypt is a good thing. Russia clearly has a very different view of the region than the United States, particularly as it pertains to Iran, and I think that we should be very wary of the Russian-Egyptian relationship improving.

We should remember, by the way, that the Egyptian military supplies are, according to estimates, 52 percent U.S.-made weapons. Most of the other weapons are Russian-made weapons from the era in which the Soviet Union funded Egypt. So Egypt can pivot to Russia in that sense. It can integrate Russian weapons, and I think that is something that we should be working very hard to prevent.

Mr. WEBBER. Is it Tadros or——

Mr. TADROS. Tadros, yes.

Mr. WEBBER. Mr. Tadros, what say you?

Mr. TADROS. Yes. I would second what Dr. Trager has said, both for the fact that a close alliance with Russia would have on Egypt's regional policies, on Iran, on Syria, on other matters, but also the possibility of a Russian model in Egypt is not something that anyone should be looking for.

Mr. WEBBER. Dr. Okail?

Ms. OKAIL. Yes. I completely agree with Mr. Tadros and Dr. Trager. I mean, having—losing the opportunity of the United States having this leverage over—pushing Egypt toward a direction that aligns with the principals of democracy and freedom that is like valued in the United States would be a better, an ideal position than having to side with Russia.

Mr. WEBBER. Sure. I think it was you, Mr. Tadros, that said Egypt has no Palestinian relationship? Was that——

Mr. TADROS. I said that in the past Egypt had played a role, whenever war would break between Hamas and the State of Israel, in brokering an agreement in exchanges of prisoners, in things like this.

This relationship is no longer there as Egypt has dramatically cut its relations with Hamas, so it can no longer play this role of truce or organizer between the two.

Mr. WEBBER. Thank you. I wanted you to clarify that.

One of our questions was—suggested this popular satirist, Bassem Youssef, who is often referred to as the Jon Stewart of Egypt, having been the brunt of one of his satires—I don't know who that is—had his—anyway, this guy, Youssef, had his popular political satire show canceled.

Now, according to reports, Mr. Youssef is saying that they made this decision to self-censor in an increasingly restrictive media environment. Is that accurate? Mr. Tadros?

Mr. TADROS. I believe it is.

Mr. WEBBER. As much as you know about it.

Mr. TADROS. Yes, I believe it is. The Egyptian regime has had a very restrictive notion about what the press should and should not cover. They believe that the completely open press that existed following the Egyptian revolution is something that undermined national security and led to chaos, and, thus, they have created restrictions on freedom of the press of TV programs and others.

Mr. WEBBER. Okay. Dr. Okail, did you say that Facebook was playing a role? And is it an increasing role?

Ms. OKAIL. Well, definitely the internet, in general, is playing an important and effective role. However, yet, I mean, still, it is very limited. It doesn't affect the entire population, 90 million people. Most of them are living in poverty, and a lot has no access to the internet. And the mainstream media or the traditional media still play an important role.

However, just a point about your earlier questions about media freedom. Another structural problem with the media is not just the political ability or authority to censor the media, but it is also the inability and the lack of resources for independent media to emerge. And that is a huge problem for many of the voices that needs a platform to democratically voice their——

Mr. WEBBER. Let me real quickly to my last question. Is CAIR, C-A-I-R, Council on American-Islamic Relations, are they playing a role between the Brotherhood and Sisi? Any kind of role in that?

Mr. TRAGER. I don't believe so. There is certainly no reports that I am aware of that——

Mr. WEBBER. None of that you know of.

Mr. TADROS. Yes. I don't believe that they are. They have been declared a terrorist organization, of course, by Egypt's ally, the

United Arab Emirates. So I don't think the Egyptian regime would be open to any talk with them.

Mr. WEBBER. Dr. Okail, any knowledge?

Ms. OKAIL. I am not sure that it would be able to play a role.

Mr. WEBBER. Thank you, Madam Chair.

Ms. ROS-LEHTINEN. Thank you, Mr. Webber.

Mr. Cicilline.

Mr CICILLINE. Thank you, Madam Chairman.

Thank you to the panelists. I hope that we can all agree that U.S. policy toward Egypt over the past few decades has had some significant flaws. We propped up an unpopular repressive dictator who abused his people at the expense of his political cronies and watched on the sidelines as the Egyptian people finally rose up against his repressive regime.

And as I listened to this testimony and I reviewed the materials that were submitted, I have become even more concerned that we are very quickly forgetting about this past and preparing to repeat history for the sake of stability, as we said, over these past many years.

And my first question to the panel is whether there are any discernible differences between the current policies toward President al-Sisi's government and our previous policies toward the Mubarak regime? Have we learned anything? I understand we have restructured, as we say, our security assistance, but have we truly evaluated the mistakes of the past and adjusted our policies for the future?

Mr. TRAGER. Thank you for your question. I would argue here that we are not propping up the current government of Egypt. That government emerged from a series of circumstances that are intrinsic to that country's domestic politics, namely the fallout from the Morsi era and strong popular support for the current type of regime.

The second lesson that I think we should draw from the previous 4 years that you referenced doesn't necessarily pertain to the extent to which the U.S. should or should not, you know, support democracy or privilege the military relationship, but it should be an analytical lesson which is that the key player in Egypt has been and will likely remain the Egyptian military. And, in that sense, the United States has made a wise choice with its partnerships.

Now, it is not an uncomplicated relationship. It is a relationship that we should be using to communicate our displeasure with Egypt's current trajectory, and we should in no way whitewash that trajectory. But, at the same time, that relationship is very important for U.S. strategy in the region.

Mr CICILLINE. Mr. Tadros or Dr. Okail?

Mr. TADROS. I think there are differences. As Dr. Trager mentioned, the United States is not completely supportive of the Sisi regime, the same way that could be said of the earlier period of the Mubarak regime. When President Mubarak took over power in similar circumstances of an Islamist challenge existing following Sadat's assassination, there were no objections from the United States to any policies that Egypt was doing.

The administration has highlighted a number of areas of dis-agreement with the regime and has been publicly expressing its displeasure with a variety of the regime's policies.

Mr CICILLINE. Dr. Okail?

Ms. OKAIL. I agree with Mr. Tadros and Dr. Trager. But I think the main difference is the realization that right now, I mean, what was—with the situation under Mubarak is that the United States wanted to make sure that the stability continues and avoid the scary scenario of having the Islamists taking power.

Right now, we are not having—we are not seeing policies that would avoid the repetition of this scenario because after the fall of Mubarak there was a vacuum where there are no secular political parties able to organize and run competitively in the elections against the Islamists.

Right now, we don't have—we don't see signs of learning from this lesson where there are no support for having political parties organized under open and democratic laws that actually allow for them to have the resources and ability and freedom to organize and be there when and if there is a challenge between them and the Islamists.

Mr. CICILLINE. So the last two things I want to ask about are the status of preparations for parliamentary elections. Have voters been allowed to register? Are parties and candidates beginning to register? Is there any real indication that these elections will in fact be held this year?

And then, secondly, what is the current status of press freedom in the country? We have heard a lot about the targeting of users of social media and bloggers, but are there any independent news-papers or TV channels that are operating? And are government-run papers and stations still engaged in this persistent kind of smear campaign against civil society and the United States?

Ms. OKAIL. Well, the process has already begun in preparing for the elections before the constitutional court decision, and registra-tion was underway and political parties were preparing for the elections.

Right now, it is on pause waiting for the new electoral, which will actually affect the way those political parties will run and cam-paign for the elections. And it is very related to your second ques-tion about the press freedom, because this is very important, and it is the only channel that would reach the masses of the people when they campaign and present themselves to the Egyptians and their voters.

Right now, the press is undergoing a lot of restrictions. As I men-tioned earlier, there are the political restrictions that actually lead people to either censor themselves because of the intimidation and fear of the prosecution, but there is also the economic restriction because the new young and independent voices, they would have the talent and ability to voice their messages, but they don't have the platform or the economic ability to actually turn that into ac-tual reality.

Thank you.

Mr CICILLINE. Thank you.

I thank the chair, and I yield back.

Ms. ROS-LEHTINEN. Thank you, Mr. Cicilline.

Dr. Yoho.

Mr. YOHO. Thank you, Madam Chair. It has been an interesting meeting here. I appreciate all the information that has come out. I have got a whole list of questions here.

The first one is, what is the credibility of the U.S. and Egypt today versus, say, 10 or 15 years ago? Dr. Trager?

Mr. TRAGER. Well, I mean, in terms of the popular perception in Egypt, the popular perception in the United States is significantly diminished because of this perception that the United States is interfering in Egypt's domestic politics. And I want to emphasize that that is not in any way my view.

Mr. YOHO. I understand.

Mr. TRAGER. But that is the perception, and it is another factor and the reason why it is so hard to influence this country's domestic politics.

Mr. YOHO. Mr. Tadros?

Mr. TADROS. I absolutely agree. The U.S. has no credibility at the moment with either side of the conflict in Egypt. The Muslim Brotherhood supporters believe that it is supporting the regime, and vice versa.

Mr. YOHO. Dr. Okail?

Ms. OKAIL. I agree. I mean, the credibility of the United States has usually been undermined throughout the 4 years of the—since the 2011 revolution. And I think, again, that is because that relationship remains a government-to-government relationship without actually transferring and conveying the message to the Egyptian people themselves and addressing their grievances.

Mr. YOHO. Okay. And I talk to people from all over the Middle East when they come here, and I hear the same thing: The U.S. has lost its credibility, and the goodwill that we have generated over the last 200 years, it is gone.

And let me ask you this. Should the U.S. have acknowledged the overthrow of Morsi as a coup? Because I know other nations have, and I think history will record it. And, if so, should we have responded in the way our laws say that no foreign aid goes to Egypt?

And I bring this up strictly because we have lost our credibility. Our word doesn't mean anything. And if we are a nation of laws and we have these policies in place, if we don't stand by that and acknowledge that, people aren't going to take us seriously. And if we had it, it may have changed the outcome in Egypt. They may have thought differently.

What is your opinion?

Mr. TRAGER. Well, I think U.S. credibility doesn't rest on the terms that we use to refer to events in Egypt. It really hinges on our relationships, and that is really where I think the loss of credibility with the current Egyptian government is. That government asks, where does the United States stand? You know, and the type of hedging that Mr. Tadros referred to has undercut our credibility not only with the current government but with both sides. And that doesn't hinge so much on what we would have called Morsi's ouster.

Mr. YOHO. Okay. Mr. Tadros, I want to ask you a separate question. Since Morsi was elected by the people democratically, would that have changed what we see today, if we would have announced that as a coup and say, "We stand with a democratic process"? Because we are promoting democracy. And since he was democratically elected, should we have intervened and said, "You can't do that; that is a coup"? I mean, what is your opinion on that?

Mr. TADROS. I don't think it—I don't believe it would have influenced the decision of the Egyptian military. The Egyptian people, there were mass protests in Egypt. People were fed up with the Muslim Brotherhood rule for a variety of reasons. And U.S. words would not have stopped the country's movement in that direction, no matter what the——

Mr. YOHO. The Arab Spring would have happened anyway.

Dr. Okail, I have a question for you. If Morsi has his death sentence carried out, what do you see happening in Egypt and the neighboring countries?

Ms. OKAIL. Well, I don't believe they actually will execute the death sentence. However, of course there will be a lot of concerns. Just after the verdict on Saturday, there were 20 terror attacks, and that is most likely in reaction to the verdict.

Again, with the interconnectivity of the transnational connection between the groups, it may trigger further coordinated attacks, and have like dire effects in general. However, we are not sure how would that like fare out.

Mr. YOHO. Okay. And then I want to build on Mr. Rohrabacher's and Mr. Webber's question about Russia's help in that region. I heard what you are saying from our perspective. What is the perspective in Egypt? What are they saying? Is Russia welcome there and looking at that, Dr. Trager?

Mr. TRAGER. Well, you know, ahead of this kind of warming of relations with Russia, the Egyptian media started speaking very, very favorably of Russia, very favorably of Putin, and I think the popular view in Egypt is that Russia is an uncomplicated relationship because they could buy weapons from Russia and Russia won't worry about the democratic issues that we are rightly raising here today.

There is one problem with that analysis within Egypt, which is that Russia isn't giving these weapons away for free. It is not offering the type of aid the United States is offering. But certainly in the short run Egypt is able to find other funds for buying Russian weapons, and they have shown that they can replace the United States, at least in the short-term withholdings.

Mr. YOHO. All right. I have one more question, but I am out of time.

Ms. ROS-LEHTINEN. Go ahead.

Mr. YOHO. Okay. Thank you, Madam Chair.

Whoever wants to answer this. Is a democracy possible without property rights acknowledged by a government in the protection of human rights as we believe here, life, liberty, and the pursuit of happiness, you know, with, you know, freedom of religion, freedom of speech? Do you see that possible in a country where we keep trying to promote a democracy without that government acknowledging those rights?

Ms. OKAIL. Well, at least the 30 years' rule of Mubarak proved that this is not possible, that——

Mr. YOHO. I agree.

Ms. OKAIL [continuing]. I mean, the whole—the entire assumptions upon which Mubarak was supported is that he is able to maintain stability, and the human rights violation and the closure of the political space could be overlooked for the sake of security and stability.

But it was proven that after like three decades of strong rule he fell in only 18 days. So, I mean, nothing would be maintained. Security solutions are essential and important, but they are not sustainable without real structural changes.

Mr. YOHO. I agree. Does anybody else——

Mr. TADROS. Yes. If I may add, no, democracy cannot be sustained without property rights, without religious freedom, and this is why the United States should not only focus on the question of holding elections as important, and this is, but on building institutions——

Mr. YOHO. Exactly.

Mr. TADROS [continuing]. The rule of law, property, economic freedom, and others.

Mr. YOHO. Thank you.

Ms. ROS-LEHTINEN. Thank you, Dr. Yoho.

Ms. Frankel.

Ms. FRANKEL. Thank you, Madam Chair. This is a very interesting discussion, and I have thought of—I have taken both sides of these issues so many times. But it just seems to me that the Arab Spring has turned into a very, very cold winter all over the world. And I think it is quite obvious that you cannot snap you fingers and get democracy and freedom and end repression.

And as much as that is our values here, and we would like to see that happen, what it sounds to me like what is happening is that we have a—you can just tell from all the questions here there is this conflict between whether or not it is—is it security versus democracy?

So a couple questions. First of all, can you say, what do you think is in our sphere of influence? And what is not? And where should our priorities be? Should it be the security of the region? I mean, what—maybe you could mention—this is an elementary question, but why is it important, or do you think it is important that Egypt be stable? And should we maybe sacrifice or turn our head on what are obvious human right abuses in order to have security?

And I would like to know, if you have time, whether you think there is a threat of ISIL or any other terrorist situation coming into Egypt.

And, finally, Madam Chair, I know I am—so if there is time——

Ms. ROS-LEHTINEN. No problem.

Ms. FRANKEL [continuing]. Whether this coup law, I will call it the coup law, needs to be changed, because it just seems to me that we are just playing with words or having to play with words in defining what happened in Egypt when al-Sisi took over.

Mr. TRAGER. Well, just in terms of what is and is not in our sphere of influence, you know, my view is that the role of foreign policy is primarily to shape the way states behave externally, and that it is often difficult to shape the way states behave internally, and that is certainly the case in the current situation in Egypt where you have the government and the Muslim Brotherhood locked in a "kill or be killed" struggle, one that the current government is winning but one that is likely to continue in some shape or form for a while.

And we can influence Egypt's external relations if we reinforce the military-to-military relationship, if Congress urges the administration to move forward with a strategic dialogue with the Egyptian government, and there are many areas in which Cairo and Washington can better coordinate, for example, in Libya.

The administration and Cairo are on very different pages there. Egypt has been, you know, the target of attacks that we believe emanate from the instability in Libya. It has responded, reportedly, by launching airstrikes in coordination with the UAE and was criticized by the administration for that, which doesn't really help the relationship because from Egypt's perspective they are attacking imminent threat.

So we need to better coordinate our policy on Libya. And, frankly, we could be doing a lot to help bolster Egypt's counterterrorism in the Sinai. That also requires the Egyptian government approving that. They have been a little bit resistant to that as the relationship has fallen on difficult times. But I think by reinvigorating the relationship we might be able to get on the same page there as well.

Mr. TADROS. I would slightly disagree. I think our sphere of influence of the United States is not only limited to foreign affairs but also to domestic ones, as long as those areas are not life-threatening to President Sisi or the regime.

The United States in the past has helped Soviet Jews. Despite that being a domestic affair in the Soviet Union, it was able to influence the fate of those people because it was not a life-threatening issue. In those areas where the regime claims or proclaims its willingness to work on them, such as religious freedom, we should hold it to task and ask it to take meaningful steps and not just symbolic gestures.

President Sisi should be encouraged to pass a law to allow the building of churches in Egypt. That is not something that threatens the stability of the country as a whole.

In terms of the ISIS threat, I think on the long run the threat from the Sinai is likely to be contained. The more alarming threat would be the growth of or the spread of violence from Libya in Egypt. The western desert is the area that voted most heavily for an Islamist candidate in all successive elections. It is 1,000 kilometers of borders with Libya, free flow of weapons from there, tribal ties to the tribes of Libya, there are many elements there that would make potential insurgency there much more threatening than the Sinai.

Ms. FRANKEL. Can Dr. Okail answer, Madam Chair?

Ms. ROS-LEHTINEN. No problem.

Ms. OKAIL. There is certainly a threat from ISIL to Egypt. And as I mentioned in my testimony, there is already one terror group. Ansar Bayt al-Maqdis have declared their loyalty to ISIS, and they got the blessing from their leader.

At the same time, there are several Egyptians who travel to Iraq, Syria, and Libya to fight there. Some of them come back home. We don't have actual numbers and information about how many there are, but they are definitely a real and existential threat to the security in the country.

As for your question concerning the support for human rights and whether we can forego that for security, I don't think that they are mutually exclusive. I think they complement each other.

And with regards to your related questions about what is in this sphere of the United States, the United States is already providing the needed support for—in terms of the military assistance. However, there is so much that can be done, particularly with regards to education reform, health support, rule of law, because so far most of the relationship and the policies targets—not just from the United States, but foreign policy in general, is having a very short-term view.

When we look at the region, when you look at Egypt in particular, out of the 90 million people, a huge percentage of this are youth under 25 years old. These are the ones that we would like to invest in, so that we would not be faced in a situation where in the next elections people will be told that if they vote for a particular party they will be voting for God, and people would buy into that and support that.

So we would like to avoid a situation of short-term policies and have long-term vision and investment in the actual people who will be shaping the future of the country.

Thank you.

Ms. Ros-Lehtinen. Thank you very much.

Thank you, Ms. Frankel.

Mr. Boyle.

Mr. Boyle. Thank you. And, first, I just want to say specifically to Dr. Okail, as one of the 43 NGO workers who physically was captured and jailed for the work that you were doing, I just great admire and deeply respect your work and the sacrifices that you yourself made.

My question is something regarding very specific and very recent. I was very concerned with not just Morsi but over 100 now being sentenced from the political opposition to death, to execution. And while certainly no fan whatsoever of the Muslim Brotherhood or of Morsi, my question is, a) what is the timeline—what does the timeline seem like in terms of the executions? Particularly with Morsi.

And then, number two, to what extent could this have a destabilizing effect? Because you only need to look at other historical examples of executions end up triggering a response in the population that ends up having a destabilizing effect. So those two questions.

Ms. Okail. Thank you so much for your kind words. I really appreciate it.

Concerning the executions, we would like—I would like to put this into the broader context. These are not the first death sentence that were issued. There were hundreds before, and for a variety of factions and people. And there are thousands of people who are in prison.

Whether these sentences will be actually implemented and executed or not, this is remaining to be seen. Highly likely they will not be. However, actually, this is another concerning point because the fact that there are verdicts that are being issued, and people have the knowledge and the acknowledgement that they will not be executed, this is an undermining of the rule of law as itself as a tool for justice, and turning it from a tool to justice into a tool for intimidation, which will actually harm the future of the Egyptian sphere of political development, social, and economic justice that people would like to see and having the law performing its role, and rather become highly politicized and highly—and more increasingly used as a tool of intimidation rather than a tool for justice. Thank you.

Mr. TADROS. I believe from the Egyptian government's time or point of view they believe that passing those death sentences against such symbolic figures as President Morsi, as the former—or the leader of the Brotherhood, General Guide Badie, and others, they are sending a message that there are no red lines, that previous Egyptian governments had shied away from arresting people like the General Guide, that even Nasser, in his repression, did not hang the General Guide.

The message from the government is that we are in this until the end. We are willing to take all necessary steps. And from their point of view, they believe that this might discourage some people from taking up arms and violence now that they realize that there are no red lines completely.

Mr. TRAGER. I agree with what has been said. I would just add that we also have to understand the death sentence is in terms of the ongoing power struggle, specifically in this case between the judiciary and the Muslim Brotherhood. That goes back almost 2 years, actually almost 3 years, excuse me, and so, I mean, I think the sentences, you know, pertain to that, which is not in any way a justification, just reinforcing that this is an ongoing power struggle within the country that is very, very hard to shape from 6,000 miles away.

Mr. BOYLE. And I would just conclude with this—and thank you, Madam Chair—it would be ironic if, after all of this and a so-called Arab Spring and all of this tumult, what ends up emerging in Egypt is a fairly pro-Western, autocratic leader that isn't very fond of the rule of law or human rights. Sounds a lot like a guy named Mubarak that was in power for three decades. It would be a bitter irony if, after all of this, that is what essentially we are left with.

Thank you, Madam Chair.

Ms. ROS-LEHTINEN. Thank you, Mr. Boyle.

Thank you. And we certainly view Egypt as a strong and important ally, and striking that balance between security and democratic reforms, we hope they find that sweet spot.

Thank you so much. Subcommittee is adjourned.

[Whereupon, at 11:46 a.m., the subcommittee was adjourned.]

APPENDIX

MATERIAL SUBMITTED FOR THE RECORD

SUBCOMMITTEE HEARING NOTICE
COMMITTEE ON FOREIGN AFFAIRS
U.S. HOUSE OF REPRESENTATIVES
WASHINGTON, DC 20515-6128

Subcommittee on the Middle East and North Africa
Ileana Ros-Lehtinen (R-FL), Chairman

May 13, 2015

TO: MEMBERS OF THE COMMITTEE ON FOREIGN AFFAIRS

      You are respectfully requested to attend an OPEN hearing of the Committee on Foreign Affairs, to be held by the Subcommittee on the Middle East and North Africa in Room 2172 of the Rayburn House Office Building (and available live on the Committee website at http://www.ForeignAffairs.house.gov):

DATE: Wednesday, May 20, 2015

TIME: 10:00 a.m.

SUBJECT: Egypt Two Years After Morsi: Part I

WITNESSES: Eric Trager, Ph.D.
                  Esther K. Wagner Fellow
                  The Washington Institute for Near East Policy

                  Mr. Samuel Tadros
                  Senior Fellow
                  Hudson Institute

                  Nancy Okail, Ph.D.
                  Executive Director
                  Tahrir Institute for Middle East Policy

By Direction of the Chairman

COMMITTEE ON FOREIGN AFFAIRS

MINUTES OF SUBCOMMITTEE ON _____ *Middle East and North Africa* _____ HEARING

Day ___*Tuesday*___ Date _____*5/20/15*_____ Room _____*2172*_____

Starting Time __*10:00 a.m.*__ Ending Time __*11:46 a.m.*__

Recesses __*0*__ (____to ____) (____to ____) (____to ____) (____to ____) (____to ____) (____to ____)

Presiding Member(s)

Chairman Ros-Lehtinen

Check all of the following that apply:

Open Session ☑
Executive (closed) Session ☑
Televised ☑

Electronically Recorded (taped) ☑
Stenographic Record ☑

TITLE OF HEARING:

Egypt: Two Years After Morsi: Part I

SUBCOMMITTEE MEMBERS PRESENT:

Chairman Ros-Lehtinen, Reps. Chabot, Weber, DeSantis, Meadows, Yoho, Clawson, Trott, Zeldin, Deutch, Connolly, Cicilline, Meng, Frankel, and Boyle

NON-SUBCOMMITTEE MEMBERS PRESENT: *(Mark with an * if they are not members of full committee.)*

Rep. Rohrabacher

HEARING WITNESSES: Same as meeting notice attached? Yes ☑ No ☐
(If "no", please list below and include title, agency, department, or organization.)

STATEMENTS FOR THE RECORD: *(List any statements submitted for the record.)*

SFR - Rep. Connolly

TIME SCHEDULED TO RECONVENE _____
or
TIME ADJOURNED __*11:46 p.m.*__

Subcommittee Staff Director

Statement for the Record
Submitted by Mr. Connolly of Virginia

It has been two years since President Mohammed Morsi was removed from power in Egypt. In order to remain clear-eyed about a secure and democratic future in Egypt, we must acknowledge that a military-backed coup against the government of President Morsi was neither just nor expedient, and that the coup does not absolve the Morsi government of its transgressions nor inoculate it from ex post facto critique.

President Morsi's shortcomings as an Egyptian leader certainly had implications for U.S. efforts to strengthen the U.S.-Egypt alliance and create a functional democracy in Egypt. On some fronts, President Morsi seemed determined to challenge longstanding Egyptian foreign policy precedents. Iranian president Mahmoud Ahmadinejad's visit to Cairo in February 2013 was the first by an Iranian leader in three decades. However, it should be noted that shortly after taking power Morsi affirmed Egypt's 1979 peace treaty with Israel, an agreement that ended a historical pattern of violence between the two nations and brought collaboration to a relationship previously defined by conflict.

Despite being Egypt's first democratically-elected president, President Morsi had difficulty operating within the bounds of traditional democratic institutions. In November 2012, just six months after taking power, he proved unresponsive to popular unrest regarding a constitutional declaration his government issued that authorized the president to take any measures deemed necessary to preserve national unity and security.

It was those protests that culminated in the coup that toppled President Morsi's government in July 2013 when the military suspended the constitution and announced that Adly Mansour, the chief justice of the Supreme Constitutional Court, would helm a transitional government until new elections could be held.

The overthrow of Morsi's government and the subsequent election of former general and coup mastermind President Abdel Fattah el-Sisi have adversely impacted U.S.-Egypt cooperation. Despite a U.S. statute that requires assistance be cut to governments whose elected head of government is deposed by a military coup, the Administration continued U.S. assistance to Egypt by refusing to label the events of July 2013 a coup. It was Congress that raised concerns about the trajectory of Egyptian democracy and repeatedly put limiting conditions on U.S. assistance in the Consolidated Appropriations acts for FY2014 and FY2015.

Despite the Administration's March 31, 2015 announcement that it would release frozen military assistance to Egypt, concerns remain. The Secretary of State has yet to certify that Egypt is supporting a democratic transition, and we have witnessed troubling developments in the judicial system and brutal crackdowns conducted by security forces. The stream of mass death sentences handed down by Egyptian judges and the killings at al Nahda and Rabaa al Adawiya squares erode confidence in the rule of law. The recent announcement that former President Morsi has been sentenced to death has already been labeled "unjust" by the U.S. State Department, and there is little doubt that carrying out the sentence would perpetuate the cycle of repression and violence in which Egypt is currently trapped.

Careful oversight of U.S. assistance to Egypt has been necessitated by these and similar incidents. The Government Accountability Office (GAO) recently released a report on U.S. assistance to Egypt that Chairman Ros-Lehtinen and I requested. The report found that the State Department has yet to conduct a long-delayed evaluation of security assistance to Egypt. The State Department claimed that in place of the review in Egypt it would conduct a similar evaluation in Lebanon as part of an effort to create a global framework for reviews of security assistance. However, Congress has subsequently been notified that the review in Lebanon is on hold, and the entire effort has been delayed once again. We must be increasingly vigilant that U.S. provided assistance is not used to further stifle freedom of expression in Egypt, and completing the evaluation in Egypt could help the U.S. accomplish broader goals, namely support for democratic governance.

Egypt is not yet the democratic success story for which we all hoped after President Hosni Murbarak's resignation. The transition has been volatile, and has suffered setbacks at times. However, if we believe that a democratic Egypt is best for region's future, U.S. policy should reflect a stern commitment to support for democratic institutions. The courts cannot serve political ends, and security forces must be trained to respect human rights. Civil society should be allowed to flourish, not stamped out as was the case when 43 employees from Freedom House, International Republican Institute, National Democratic Institute, and International Center for Journalists were convicted of operating unregistered NGOs by an Egyptian court in June 2013.

As the second largest recipient of U.S. military assistance and a major non-NATO ally, Egypt has long undergirded our security strategy in the Middle East. I welcome our witnesses to share their perspectives on the direction of Egyptian democracy, and suggestions for how the U.S. can facilitate a secure and stable Egypt.